# Brooklyn Rapid Transit Trolley Lines In Queens

## By
## Vincent F. Seyfried

## N.J. International Inc.
## 1998

# Index

| Page | |
|---|---|
| 2 | Introduction |
| 3 | Old Williamsburgh |
| 5 | Grand St. In The 60's & 70's |
| 9 | Palmy Days Of The Grand St. & Newtown R.R. 1880-1890 |
| 16 | Metropolitan Ave. |
| 24 | The Corona, Fresh Pond And Flushing Ave. Extension |
| 27 | Cypress Hills & Lutheran Lines In Ridgewood |
| 35 | Electrification Of Grand St. And Extension To North Beach |
| 38 | The Dummy Comes To Richmond Hill |
| 39 | High Finances & Hot Fighting |
| 41 | Metropolitan Ave. In The 90's |
| 44 | Brooklyn City R.R. Reaches Flushing |
| 48 | Recovery & Expansion 1895-1900 |
| 54 | North Side Lines 1900-1917 |
| 59 | Myrtle Ave. & Cypress Hills 1895-1917 |
| 64 | Hard Times & Receivership 1918-1923 |
| 70 | The Last Years 1923-1948 |
| 74 | Review Of Final Operations |
| 88 | Roster |

# INTRODUCTION

Nearly forty years have passed since the original version of this book first appeared in 1959. The original edition was limited to approximately 700 copies and specimens today are hard to come across. A whole new generation of trolley enthusiasts has grown up since 1948 when the last BRT traction line vanished from the streets of Queens and few of this new group have ever seen the original edition or had a chance to read its pages.

To serve this new audience and give new life to the long and fascinating pageant of street car history provides the main motive for this revised re-issue of a nostalgic volume. The text has been somewhat abridged and photo selection emphasis has changed from locations to car types and operations. A BRT general roster is included plus the original maps.

Garden City, N.Y.  *Vincent F. Seyfried*
August, 1996

# OLD WILLIAMSBURGH

The traveler passing through Brooklyn of today observes in every part of the borough a seemingly endless vista of apartment houses, small factories, private homes, and neighborhood stores. There is no visble break in the line of buildings and little variation in style, other than the obvious difference in prosperity that differentiates the blighted area from the newer and well-to-do neighborhoods. Despite this homogeneous appearance of today, Brooklyn, as we know it, can scarcely be said to be more than a century old. If one were to turn back the clock to the 40's and 50's of the last century, the two original settlements out of which Brooklyn developed would be very apparent.

The first and oldest of these was the area around Fulton Ferry which contained several small Dutch settlements, one of which, Breukelen, gave its name to the city of today. The Fulton Ferry was the oldest traditional gateway to Long Island, and from it radiated, even in colonial times, the highways and turnpikes that gave access to the inland villages of Bedford, Midwood, Flatbush, Jamaica, etc.

The second of these two original settlements lay north of the present Navy Yard constituting the present areas of Williamsburgh and Greenpoint. Though Fulton Ferry developed into a substantial commercial and residential village as early as the 17th century, Williamsburgh did not achieve the status of a village till the early 19th century. At the time of the American Revolution, all of the present Williamsburgh and Greenpoint had long since been parceled out into farms worked by descendants of the original Dutch settlers. The names of these men are familiar to us from the later streets named after them: Meserole, Boerum, Remsen, Wyckoff, Titus, Vandervoort and Troutman. Along the shore and in the low lying areas dense thickets existed.

During the Revolution when times were hard, the British and American soldiers, encamped on the Long Island shore, cut down these thickets for fuel, and so cleared large areas for future settlement. By 1800, new farms and orchards were established on the cleared lands and began to crowd the old Dutch farms which were frequently sold and sub-divided. Shipping produce from these early farms gave rise to the roads and ferries leading to New York. In 1802 the first settlement was laid out and named Williamsburgh after the man who surveyed it, Col. Jonathan Williams. By 1827 the village had grown sufficiently to be incorporated and stretched from Newtown Creek to Division Avenue (now Broadway), so called because it divided Williamsburgh from Brooklyn. There were three main streets: the Shore Road (Kent Avenue); N. 2nd Street (Metropolitan Avenue); and the newest road, Grand Street.

Such, in brief, is the early history of the area that forms the subject of our story. What sort of town was the Williamsburgh of this period? It was but natural that the busiest and most thickly populated section lay along the waterfront. Connection with New York was all important. As early as 1797 a rowboat ferry operated from the foot of Grand Street to Grand Street, New York. This became a real ferry in 1812. In the 1820's the old horse boats were supplanted by steam ferries. In the 50's and 60's additional boats left Grand Street for Peck Slip and Roosevelt Street, New York. About 1810 a ferry began operations from the foot of Metropolitan Avenue. In time four ferries left from here, to Roosevelt St., Grand St., 23rd St. and 42nd St. All the ferries charged 2 or 3 cents. With the passing of the years, the ferries became the main factor in building up the Williamsburgh area, or Eastern District as it came to be known.

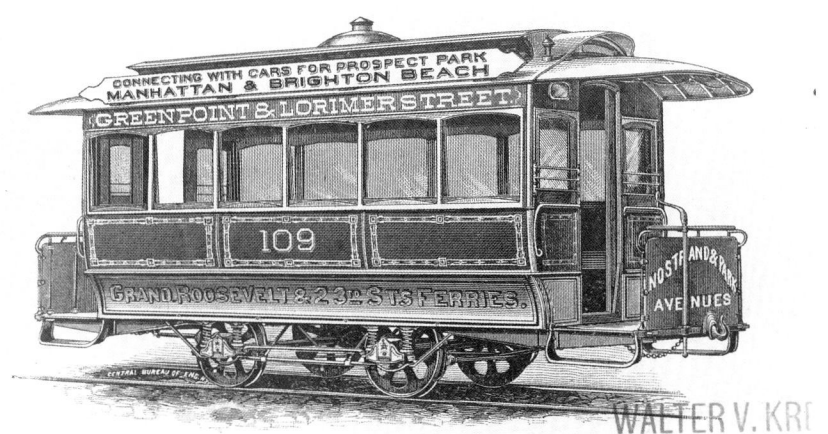

Typical horse car of the Greenpoint & Lorimer R.R. Co. Built by Louis & Fowler Car Co. 1886. *Edward Watson collection.*

In the 1820's and 30's N. 2nd St. was the main artery, but with the opening of Grand St. in 1812, the latter gradually became the principal business street. Grand St. really typified old Williamsburgh. Row upon row of neat two story wooden houses lined its sides; with the rapid development of business in the 50's, the houses were often moved into the yard, and store fronts lined the streets in increasing numbers. This was the day of the individual craftsman, and the many products needed for the expanding city gave rise to small stores and small factories. The first newspaper appeared in the 40's, and these vigorously advertised the commercial emporiums of Grand St. Here H. C. Bohack opened his first grocery store in 1888; Lord & Taylor maintained an elegant establishment on Grand St.; and the original Atlantic & Pacific Tea Co. did business at Rodney St.

On Grand St. near Kent Ave. several hotels did a thriving business catering to travelers on their way into Long Island, and to salesmen and farmers who were attracted to Williamsburgh as a good locality for drumming up trade.

Much of the prosperity of old Williamsburgh lay in its excellent communications with Queens County and the rest of Long Island. At the end of the Revolutionary War there were scarcely any roads connecting the East River waterfront with the interior villages. This defect was rapidly remedied by the sudden and spectacular growth of the turnpikes.

In 1809 the old Indian trail from Fulton Ferry to Jamaica opened as the Brooklyn, Jamaica and Flatbush Turnpike Co. In the Williamsburgh area public streets had been laid out early, but where the open fields began beyond Bushwick Ave. and north of Newtown Creek, the turnpikes soon sprang up and became valuable arteries of trade and commerce. The next important turnpike to open was the Williamsburgh & Jamaica Turnpike in 1814. This is the present Metropolitan Ave. The road began at the present intersection of Bushwick and Metropolitan Avenues and was surveyed in a straight line all the way to Jamaica. Construction took place in 1814-1816; in September 1816 the road opened for traffic. The first toll gate was at the English Kills bridge over Newtown Creek.

The Maspeth Ave. & Toll Bridge Co. was founded in 1836 and opened the present Maspeth Ave. to traffic in 1840. The road began at Bushwick and Metropolitan Avenues and crossed Newtown Creek and Furman's Island, ending at the present junction of Maspeth Ave., Maurice Ave. and 58th St. on the Queens side. Though a short road, it soon became important because it provided the only thoroughfare leading directly east toward the village of Newtown.

What is now Flushing Ave. opened as a turnpike in 1814, and was known as the Brooklyn & Newtown Plank Road. The beginning of this turnpike was the present intersection of Marcy and Park Avenues. The road then wandered diagonally across Tompkins and Throop Avenues, joining the present bed of Flushing Ave. at a point midway between Throop and Sumner Avenues. Here it continued in its present course to the present junction of Maspeth, Grand and Flushing Avenues.

If one wanted to travel to Newtown and Flushing two additional plank roads made this possible. The Newtown & Maspeth Plank Road Co. began at the terminus of the Maspeth turnpike road at the present corner of Maspeth & Maurice Avenues. It is the present Maspeth Ave. as far as the corner of Grand St. and Flushing Ave., then it became the present Grand St. all the way out to the present Queens Blvd.

Brooklyn Rapid Transit open trolley No.1417.

Here it joined old Broadway in Newtown village. At the end of Broadway where Elmhurst Ave. intersects it, began the Flushing & Newtown Road & Bridge Co. This carried the traveler over the present bed of Elmhurst Ave. all the way to Flushing Bridge.

Such were the main avenues of communication leading east from old Williamsburgh into Queens. Two turnpikes led north over Newtown Creek into the present Long Island City. The Greenpoint & Flushing Plank Road was built in 1853-54 from Greenpoint Ferry on the East River to Calvary Cemetery with a bridge over the creek. More important was the Newtown & Bushwick Turnpike. This began at "Penny Bridge", the point where Laurel Hill Blvd. touched Newtown Creek. The turnpike then ran along the present Laurel Hill Blvd. and 45th Avenue to old Broadway in Newtown village, where the Flushing & Newtown Turnpike began. Because a large part of the road was graded with crushed oyster shells, it became known as Shell Road. The road opened in 1836 and built a bridge across Newtown Creek on stone piers and charged 1 cent to walk across; hence the name Penny Bridge. The present Meeker Ave. led from Penny Bridge into old Williamsburgh.

The phenomenal growth and prosperity of old Williamsburgh and the excellent communications with the villages of Queens to the east and north soon created a demand for some sort of public transit. The two principal commercial arteries where such transit was needed were Grand St. and N. 2nd St., the Williamsburgh continuation of Metropolitan Ave. The transit line on each of these streets is a story in itself and will be taken up separately.

# GRAND STREET IN THE 60'S & 70'S

Local transit in the middle of the 19th century became regularised in the form of stage coach routes. These grew up in Williamsburgh in the 1840's and 50's and radiated out from the Grand St. Ferry. The principal traffic on this route was to Calvary Cemetery. The Roman Catholic Archdiocese of New York had purchased the old Alsop farm along the north banks of Newtown Creek and inland, and in 1848 dedicated the tract as Calvary Cemetery. Almost all burials were those of residents of Manhattan, and traffic to the cemetery of relatives and mourners passed entirely through Williamsburgh, making a lucrative traffic.

When the new horse railroads established in Manhattan in the 50's proved to be a success, Williamsburgh decided on a street railway venture of its own. The franchise was granted and on August 18, 1860 the Grand St. & Newtown R.R. Co. was incorporated to build a double track railroad,"from the easterly side of First St. (Kent Ave.) . . . to the village of Newtown in Queens," also along "Grand St. from First St. to Bushwick Ave. and thence through said Bushwick Ave. to Maspeth Ave. to the village of Newtown." Though both these routes envisaged a line to Newtown, it was destined not to be built until 1876 chiefly because the Maspeth Ave. & Toll Bridge Co., owner of the only road leading to Newtown, stood in the way. The company decided, therfore, not to attempt to reach Newtown village until Grand St. itself should be extended into Queens.

Since the stage line to Calvary Cemetery paid well, the horse railway company apparently bought out the franchise and laid tracks along the old stage route. On Monday, October 15, 1860, the Grand St. line opened. The road had been completed from from Kent Ave. to Bushwick Ave., at that time the end of the street. The new cars that had been ordered failed to arrive on time, and the franchise would have lapsed had the company not begun operation immediately, so three Brooklyn City horse cars were borrowed for the occasion from the Court St. line. The legend "Grand St. and Bushwick Ave." was painted on strips of muslin and stretched over "Greenwood via Court Street". On Tuesday, the 16th, regular service began on a 3 cent fare.

As a temporary measure the new company erected large wooden buildings at the corner of Grand & Humboldt Streets for use as stables. Within a week the first four cars arrived from Eaton, Gilbert & Co. of Troy, N.Y., and were put in service on October 29th; each car cost $850, a very high figure for that day. Arrangements were made with the Brooklyn City R. R. to run down Kent Ave. on their tracks to Broadway Ferry. Here the new company purchased property on the west side of Kent Ave. just above Broadway for the erection of a brick building containing an office and waiting room.

The company steadily increased its cars as well as its horses during these years: in 1867 there were 15: in 1869, 19, the car horses went from 88 in 1867 to 99 in 1869. Traffic was heavy for a horse car line only 40 blocks long: half a million a year in 1861, and nearly a million and a half annually during 1866-1870, an indication of the density of population in old Williamsburgh. The exact figures are as follows:

| 1861 | 533,426 | 1864 | 830,798 | 1867 | 1,446,800 |
| 1862 | 521,764 | 1865 | 1,128,614 | 1868 | 1,202,659 |
| 1863 | 676,634 | 1866 | 1,359,218 | 1869 | 1,341,304 |
|      |         |      |         | 1870 | 1,368,268 |

The trip from the Grand St. ferry to Calvary Cemetery took 31 minutes. The cars were painted yellow and at night carried a green light. The main car barn and depot of the company was on the south side of Meeker Ave. between North Henry and Monitor Streets.

Early in 1870 a few improvements were undertaken: all new rails for the stretch between Union and Bushwick Avenues; nine new cars were also bought in May. Beginning with December 29, 1870 the Board of Directors decided to run all night cars for the first time on Grand St. "for the accommodation of the numerous printers working on New York dailies and others who labor during night hours." For some reason this owl service was stopped after a few months but was resumed on May 15, 1871.

In the year 1870 the Grand St. & Newtown R.R. Co. bought a part of another street surface line for $20,000. It happened that in the year before (1869) the Metropolitan R.R. then operationg along Metropolitan Ave. to Middle Village, had fallen into bankruptcy. It was sold at auction by the Sheriff and bought in by the Mechanics National Bank of Syracuse, N.Y. by its president Austin Meyer. Meyers appears to have broken the property into two lots. The Williamsburgh half of the line west of Bushwick Ave. he reorganized into a new company. The eastern half from Bushwick Ave. to the Lutheran Cemetery entrance in Middle Village he sold to the Grand St. & Newtown R.R.

The Grand St. & Newtown R.R. applied for and received a franchise from the Legislature to operate out to Middle Village. The company was authorized to "lay a double track on Grand St. from its present tracks on the corner of Bushwick Ave. to Metropolitan Ave.; thence through Metropolitan Ave. to the Lutheran Cemetery in Queens.

The Lutheran Cemetery extension east from Bushwick Ave. totaled three miles and the trip from the ferry took 50 minutes. The operation of this line required an increase in rolling stock,

27 cars being listed in 1870 and 32 in 1871. Since both the Metropolitan and Grand St. companies were operating out to the Lutheran Cemetery, the traffic was necessarily divided between them, and neither company could have met expenses. The line was profitably patronized only on Sundays in the summer season. After only two seasons the Grand St. company decided to abandon its new branch, and on April 4, 1873 sold back to Meyers the road it had bought from him in 1870. Thereafter Grand St. cars terminated their runs at the Newtown Creek bridge.

In 1874 the company built new general offices and a two-track terminal on the northwest corner of Kent Ave. and Broadway at No.394. The Broadway ferry was then extremely busy: four different ferries operated out of the slip to Grand St. N.Y., Roosevelt St., and 42nd Streets. For the first time it became possible to get the cars off the congested street and into a "car stand" on private property.

The year 1876 was a banner year for the company as the old dream of reaching Newtown, a goal since early 1860, was finally achieved. Up to 1876 no road led from Williamsburgh directly east toward Newtown, except Maspeth Ave. owned by the turnpike company.

We have previously mentioned the fact that the Maspeth turnpike company declined to permit the Grand St. & Newtown R.R. to use its road to reach Newtown. The reason for this was the Maspeth Ave. company's own prospect of laying rails and running its own horse car line; the Legislature had been petitioned for permission to engage in such railroad activities and the company had received permission to merge itself with its specially created railroad subsidiary, called the Williamsburgh & Newtown R.R. Co., previously incorporated on February 14, 1866. The franchise permitted the Maspeth turnpike company to run a horse railroad from Broadway Ferry up Kent Ave. and N. 2nd St. to Bushwick Ave. and then along Maspeth Ave. turnpike over Newtown Creek and through Queens to the present Grand St. (then the Newtown & Maspeth Plank Road Co.) then along Grand St. to Newtown. The route was actually laid with the best imported iron rails in 1867 as far east as Maiden Lane (now Mazeau St.). Just as the road company was getting ready to operate, the Brooklyn city officials seized the Brooklyn end of Maspeth Ave. for a public highway and raised the grade. Rather than go to the expense of raising the tracks to the new grade, the turnpike company tore up the rails in July and August 1873 and sold them for $65 a ton to the Broadway R.R. Co. With the withdrawal of the Maspeth Turnpike Co. from the field in 1873, the way was now clear for the Grand St. & Newtown R.R. to build its own line to Newtown Village.

On August 3, 1876, cars began running on a regular schedule, and time tables were posted at the depot and in the newspapers. Cars to Brooklyn moved on a 40 to 30 minute headway all day from 5 a.m. to 6:30 p.m.; cars for Newtown left the ferry on a similar headway from 6 a.m. to 7:30 p.m. Cars arriving in Newtown went up Broadway as far as the LIRR station, and then went back to the stables.

The new extension fully justified the expectations of its backers in volume of traffic. On the first Sunday there was a rush, and from early morning till the last car, every vehicle was crowded, and had there been a dozen extra cars, they would have been filled. The Newtown citizens utilized the cars going to and from church; the crowds of curious from Williamsburgh exhausted the few public eating places in little Newtown.

Both road and bridge were a great success. The horse car company added two extra trips daily. Grand St. itself became the chief thoroughfare through which the farmers of Flushing and North Hempstead and Newtown reached the markets. An almost continous procession of market wagons traveled the new road daily between 3 p.m. and midnight. All this commercial activity brought lively trade to Williamsburgh and heavy patronage to the stores, hotels and saloons along old Grand St. The opening of the new road almost destroyed traffic over the old private turnpike road on Maspeth Ave. and its bridge over Newtown creek. The owners tried to sell the franchise to the counties of King & Queens for $40,000, but neither would buy it. The franchise was due to expire in 1881, and because the bridge was old and dilapidated, the property was felt to be worthless.

One of the underlying, but seldom realized reasons for the popularity of the horse railroad, was the steam railroad situation in Newtown in the middle '70's. The Flushing & North Side R.R., then an independent company, had its Newtown depot on Broadway somewhat north of the village. The LIRR in 1873, desirous of cutting itself in on the Flushing traffic, opened its White Line branch through the heart of Newtown village. The two competing railroads undercut each other's rates repeatedly until the whole trip from Flushing to Long Island City was only 8 cents. Suddenly in 1876 this excellent situation came to an abrupt end. Both railroads fell under a common management, and rates were promptly raised to their old levels. On top of this the White Line passing through the center of Newtown village was abruptly closed down permanently in April 1876 and passengers had to walk several blocks north to the former Flushing & North Side R.R. depot. The high fare of 21 cents and the abandonment of the Newtown depot occurred just five months before the horse railroad extended into town; some of the welcome accorded the horse cars was therefore inspired by

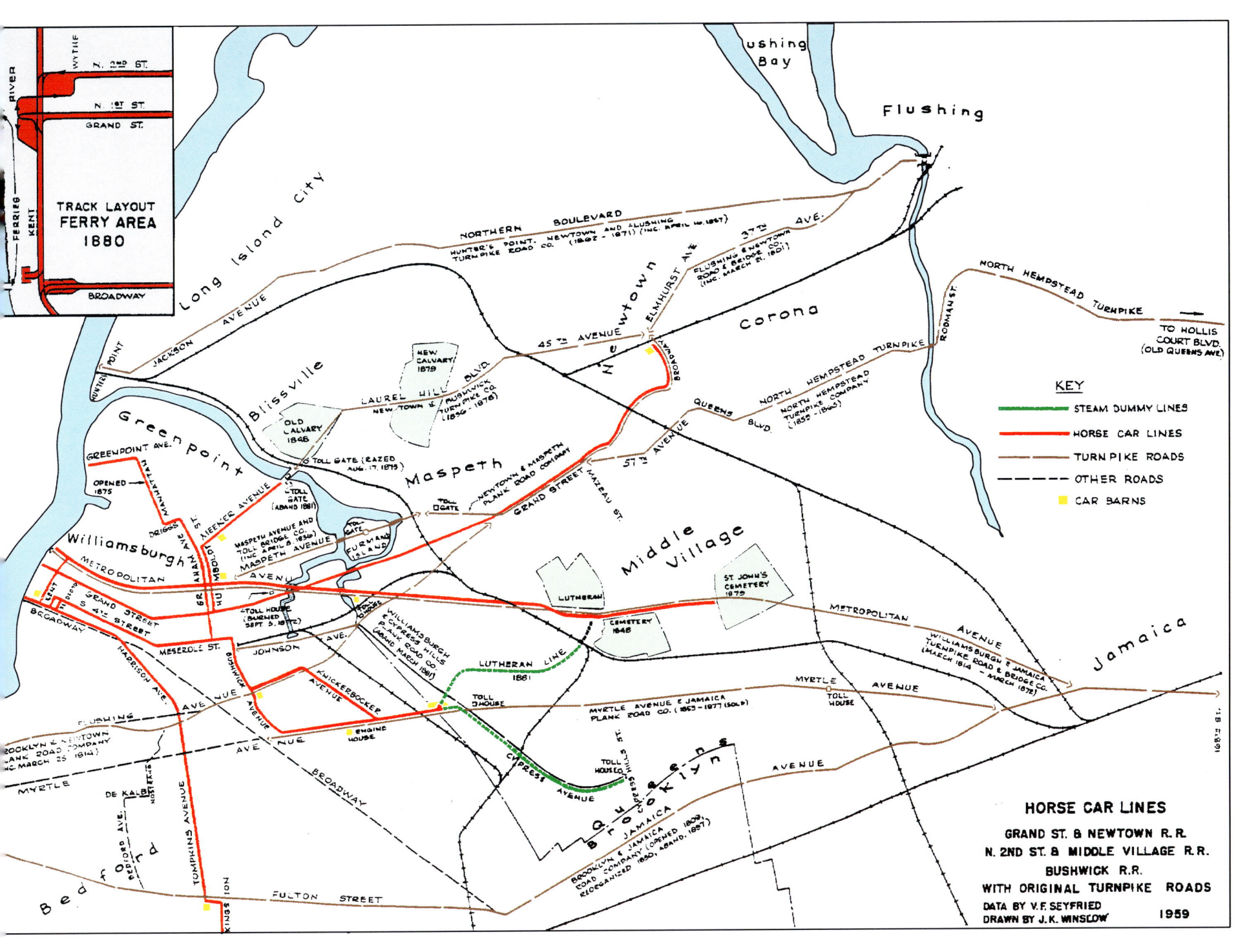

Bushwick R.R. horse car No 116 of the Tompkins Ave. line, July 1876. Built by Stephenson. *Vincent F. Seyfried collection.*

a feeling of spite and indignation against the LIRR and with the hope that the horse cars would break the LIRR's monopoly and provide a new, cheap outlet to the city.

In May 1878 the company doubled tracked a short stretch of its line from Metropolitan Ave. to some point east of the creek not named. Road conditions in 1878 were as bad as before. The Highway Commissioners and the Supervisors together appropriated $3.200 to put the avenue in complete repair.

In the spring of 1878 the Grand St. & Newtown R.R. gained additional importance by becoming a feeder to the new Manhattan Beach R.R. which opened on April 9, 1878. The new railroad had a dock at Quay St. on the East River. The line then traversed Greenpoint and crossed the Grand St. railroad twice: at Humbolt St. where there was a station, and where Grand St. intersected Metropolitan Ave. and Newtown Creek. A station was errected here also and in the summer season crowds of people boarded the trains at these two stations and others along the line for Manhattan Beach. The Grand St. horse cars acted as a natural feeder at both stations and undoubtedly gained patronage thereby. In mid-August the order was given out to all horse car drivers to come to a full stop before crossing the tracks of the Manhattan Beach R.R. and not to proceed until the conductor gave the signal to come ahead.

In the summer of 1878 the residents of Corona again agitated for horse car service, and some landowners were even willing to donate the land. In September the company again made repairs to the paving inside and outside of the rails because of the bitter complaints of farmers getting their wagons caught.

Two improvements were made at the end of the year, stoves were installed in the middle of the cars to warm passengers on the 50 minute ride into Williamsburgh, and the cars had new improved headlights installed.

With the close of the year 1879 traffic on the Grand St. & Newtown R.R. reached new heights. The heavily loaded cars at certain times of the day made it seem as if a second track all the way to Newtown were warranted. The statistics for the period 1870-1880 show a steady increase in patronage as Williamsburgh grew bigger and more important:

1871   1,982,565      1873   1,806,587      1880   1,906,244
1872   1,897,673      1874   1,796,889

Operating schedules for the horse cars were reguarly posted at the depots and possibly in the cars; they were regulary published in the newspapers. Traffic steadily rose in the late '70's and to handle the increase volume of travel, additional cars were put on and the headway shortened. When the service to Newtown began in 1876, cars had run half-hourly. By 1880 cars were running every 6 minutes to Calvary Cemetery and every 15 minutes to Newtown. As early as August 1876 it had become profitable to put on a late Saturday car (9:40 p.m.) from Newtown, returning at 10:40 p.m., and a 7:20 p.m. car on weekdays; Newtown at this period was but a small and comparatively remote village.

Both open and closed cars were used by the Grand St. R.R.. The open cars came out as early as the first week in May, and ran as late as the last week in September.

Let us take an imaginary 1880 trip from Broadway Ferry on a Grand St. horse car. Just north of the ferry buildings is the company's terminal at 394 Kent Ave.. Two tracks lead into the street floor, and we have our choice of the yellow Calvary car or the blue Newtown car.

The view at the ferry was a sight to see. Wagons hurried to and fro and passengers leaving the boats and lining up to board others crowded the sidewalks. In the street stand numerous horse cars of all shades, each line in those days sporting a different color. At night or in the rush hour of a winter's evening, an approching car was identified by the color of the bull's eye, a little round glass inserted in front of a kerosene lamp kept in a closed box in the upper right hand corner on either end of a car. So when a red, green or any other colored light came into view, it was at once known to which line the incoming car belonged. If we examine our Calvary car closely, we will notice that it bears a green light.

Boarding our yellow cemetery car, we make the trip up crowded Kent Ave. We pass on the left Havemeyer and Elder's great sugar refinery at S. 3rd St., now the home of *Domino* sugar. Between S. 5th and 6th Streets is the Williamsburgh Hotel. On either side of the street all along Kent Ave. are numerous manufacturing plants, and a few surviving homes.

As we turn into Grand St., one can see the American Hotel and the Pavilion Hotel and the Metropolitan Hotel on the southeast corner. All these housed transients coming over on the ferries, and visitors from Long Island. From Kent Ave. eastward we pass a solid line of stores and occasional banks and insurance companies, churches and houses, in short the great variety of business that a thickly settled community like Williamsburgh required. At Rodney St. was located the original A & P, and at Bedford Ave. the paint store of Daniel Maujer, a director of the company. Here was the main business section of old Williamsburgh.

As we turn up Humboldt St. dwellings greatly outnumber the stores. A few livery stables and neighborhood stores interrupt the houses here and there. Turning in Meeker Ave. stores again predominate, interrupted by saloons. At N. Henry St., we pass the car stables and soon reach Penny Bridge, the terminus. Here we dismount and pay a 1 cent toll to the gate keeper of the Newtown & Bushwick Turnpike for the privilege of crossing Newtown Creek.

Returning on the next car we can change at Humbolt and Grand Sts. for the blue Newtown car. As we approach Newtown Creek, we pass the station of the Manhattan Beach R.R. and beyond the big lumber yards of Dannatt & Pell and A.A. Newman. At this point the double track ends, and we enter single track probably on the south side of the street with turnouts at mile intervals. For a mile to the eastward of the creek there were few establishments because the avenue had been opened so recently. One industry had established itself, however, to everyone's regret. These were the fragrant bone-boiling establishments that sent out wagons daily to collect the carcasses of dead horses which were then boiled and rendered down for fertilizer. The terrible stench given off by these works insured their isolation and tortured the passengers of the Grand St. cars in the Newtown Creek section. In addition, boatloads of garbage from New York City were unloaded here and burnt on the marshes for fill.

The meadow area just east of the creek bore the name of Melvina in those days. When the horse car reached the present junction of Flushing Ave. and Grand St., the pleasent little suburban village of Columbusville began. Trim substantial houses lined Grand St. and the side streets and gradually thinned out as one moved east. Beyond Mazeau St., where North Hempstead Turnpike formerly branched off there were nothing but farms to be seen on either side of the street. Not until one approched Moore's Corner, now Queens Blvd. and Broadway, did civilization again begin. Here was the well settled village of old Newtown, with Broadway lined with shops and private homes. We cross the disused White Line branch of the LIRR at grade, and finally pull up to the car stables at Elmhurst Ave. The combined ride on both branches has consumed an hour and a half, and we are far out in the "country", for beyond Newtown the farms extend for mile on mile.

## PALMY DAYS OF THE GRAND ST. & NEWTOWN R. R. 1880-1890

In the 80's the Grand St. company attained its fullest maturity and prosperity. The extension of the avenue into Newtown channeled an increasingly heavy and profitable flow of traffic through the avenue, and converted lower Grand St. into a downtown shopping center with large department stores that compared favorably with New York in variety of goods and lavishness of display. The hard times of the 70's with their bank failures, general tightness of money, and labor unrest were over, and a new era of wealth, prosperity and expansion succeeded. The population was expanding rapidly and Brooklyn and New York shared in the general prosperity of the nation.

It is our good fortune that this golden age of the Grand St. company received unusually close and friendly scrutiny from the press of the day. The village of Newtown at the eastern end of the line was a small one-street hamlet, but on this single road was clustered in close proximity not only residences, but the company carbarn and the pressroom of the "Newtown Register". The "Register" was a country weekly featuring much local gossip. As one of the town's biggest industries, the horse railroad received its full share of publicity in the "Register" columns. When copy ran low, filler articles were easily secured by merely looking out the window toward the car depot, or by sending a reporter across the street to chat with the foreman. Thanks to this happy circumstance, the day-to-day affairs of the horse railroad pass before us in fresh and vivid detail.

At the outset of the decade, 1881, the service provided seems all that one could have asked. The most conspicuous gain in riding is reflected in the statistics for week end traffic. The picnic parks and the baseball grounds attracted record numbers of people from the city in summer and were the main cause of the company's prosperity. Queens County Park on Grand St. in Maspeth was one of these weekend attractions featuring attractive accommodations for ball players, picnickers, and dancing parties.

The largest of all the week-end retreats was Monteverde's Grand St. Park just east of Juniper Ave., opened about 1848. This place had extensive grounds, and on big week ends in July and August, 5,000 people could crowd into the park. The main attractions were ball playing on the extensive lots in the rear, and picnicking and dancing under the trees. Home-going crowds from this park alone completely filled the little horse cars from Newtown until the inside aisles and the running boards were jammed. All too often gangs of roughs from Brooklyn came to the park, got drunk and then crowded onto the Grand St. cars for the homeward ride. They jostled the patrons, and frightened ladies with their rowdyism, cursing and swearing. Often they crowded the roofs of the cars, put their feet through the windows, and defied the efforts of the conductors to collect fares. The drivers and conductors were hard put to it to keep the peace, but the superintendent and officials looked the other way so long as the nickels showered down into the coffers of the company.

It was resorts like these that fed capacity crowds to the Grand St. railroad early in the season and on every sunny summer week end thereafter. For the year 1882 we begin to get exact statistics on the number of cars required to handle the summer traffic. In June 1882 five cars ran under a 30 minute headway, but after July 4th, seven cars were put on a 20 minute headway; the extra two were the first "bobtail" cars seen on the road and used experimentally. Within a week the travel exceeded the capacity, and as the cars passed the amusement parks along the line, additional crowds stormed the little cars trying to ride home to Williamsburgh. The heavy riding continued all summer and as late as November 12 cars ran on a 10 minute headway and did an immense business. Some of the cars were specially scheduled to connect with the Manhattan Beach trains; this railroad began operations about May 30th annually, and horse cars thereafter connected with the steam trains at the Metropolitan Ave. station near the creek.

The following season - 1883 - 15 cars ran on the road as early as June and were packed on each trip. On July 15th, 14 cars made seven trips each carrying full paying loads.

Some idea of the peak loads of these early days can be gauged by the number of licenses bought from the city; in 1883 the company bought 21 car licenses at $20 apiece which seems to give us an idea of the maximum cars out in the street at any one time. The winter schedule offered almost as much accommodation. In the fall of 1883 the company was running four large closed cars plus "bobtails". These were on a 10 minute headway to 9 a. m.; then at 20 minutes to 3 p. m.; and 10 minutes again from 3 to 7 p. m. For a line with half its trackage in the suburban territory, this was good service. Seventy-three trips were being made daily between Newtown and the ferries.

The season of 1884 opened with the announcement that 14 open cars would be run during the summer at 10 minute intervals. Double-headers were considered for the first time, and an interval of 5 minutes. As early as April the 5 and 10 minute headway was implemented, two months earlier than any previous season. The road was reaching capacity and the superintendent petitioned the directors for a new building at Newtown capable of holding 100 horses. On Sunday, June 23rd, it is recorded that 6,000 people were carried on the line.

The headway by this time had been squeezed to maximum limits imposed by a single-track operation and any speed-up would require the building of additional turnouts. In February 1884 the company explored this possibility, and in April began construction. The new turnouts were located between the ones in use, and were to be spring-switches that did not require the use of hand switch-irons as did the old. By the first week of June all the new turnouts were in position and their "automatic" feature was admired by the patrons.

In the fall of the year the 10 minute schedule was restored between 7 a. m. and 7 p. m. and then lengthened to 15 minutes. By the end of 1884 it was calculated that the little horse railroad had carried an average of 7,668 passengers per day! In the year 1886, the last for which we have daily statistics, there were certain Sundays when 14,000 people were hauled.

The 80's were also the period when an "owl" service gradually developed. As early as 1881 there was a tendency to late cars, particularly on Saturday evenings for those wanting to prolong visiting in Williamsburgh until late hours, and for those wanting to attend late theatre performances. At that time a 9 p. m. car left from the ferries, and continued to run until January 1882. In May 1883 on the Meeker Avenue branch to Penny Bridge cars were scheduled to run regularly as late as 10 p.m. The year 1885 brought a demand for still later hours, and the company acceded by scheduling a 10:40 p.m. car from Newtown, leaving the ferry at 11:50 and returning to Newtown at 12:50 a.m. This was the first true "owl" service. By 1888 the population had grown sufficiently through Maspeth and Newtown to stimulate a demand for all night service.

The annual statistics reveal a steadily increasing patronage:

| | | | | | |
|---|---|---|---|---|---|
| 1881 | 2,015,496 | 1884 | 2,798,634 | 1888 | 2,929,617 |
| 1882 | 2,068,418 | 1885 | 2,791,288 | 1889 | — |
| 1883 | — | 1886 | 2,849,321 | 1890 | 2,279,002 |
| | | 1887 | 2,940,974 | | (to Oct. 31st) |

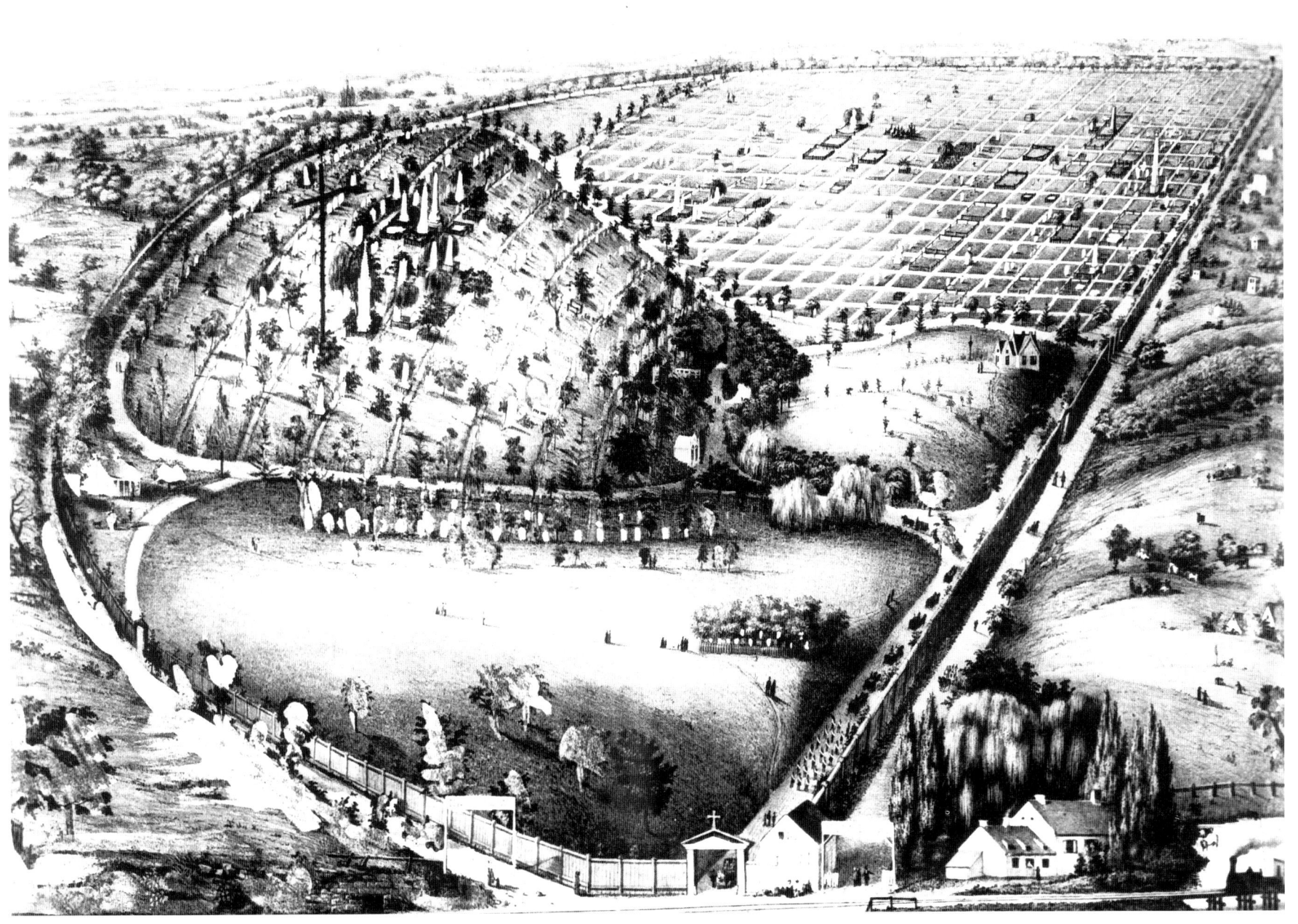

**Engraving of old Calvary Cemetery by J. Schmittt 1855.** *Vincent F. Seyfried collection.*

Traffic statistics had increased so encouragingly each year that the company became receptive to the idea of expanding into fresh territory. For many years the company had profited from the cemetery traffic to Calvary via Grand St. and Meeker Ave. In November 1883 the officials of the railroad, without asking anyone's permission, decided to lay tracks on the newly built iron draw bridge at Penny Bridge. This would permit direct service to the cemetery entrance instead of stopping at the Brooklyn side of the creek. Down to 1882 the bridge had been the private property of the Newtown & Bushwick Turnpike which charged a 1 cent toll, but the charter had expired and passage was now free to all. On the morning of October 30th a wagon load of iron rails was quietly hauled across the bridge at 7 a.m. and piled up on the Queens side. President Webb was on hand to watch as a second truck loaded with timber approached the bridge. At this point "Kit" Fagan, the bridge keeper, got wind of what was going on, forbade the driver to cross, and telephoned the superintendent of the Queens County Board of Supervisors. When he arrived on the scene, he ordered the bridge thrown open and kept open for the greater part of the day to prevent the railroad men from laying tracks. That afternoon the matter was brought up before the board and they confirmed the supervisor's action and forbade any construction. They ordered the sheriff to guard the bridge until an injunction could be obtained. In December the company formally sought and obtained permission to make a new terminus in Queens County and a turntable was constructed on the Queens side of Penny Bridge.

Sentiment in Queens County was not wholly against the railroad. The residents of Laurel Hill, a little village just east of Calvary, were delighted at the prospect of horse car service, and favored the Grand St. company provided it agreed to continue the extension to their village, half a mile farther up. They petitioned the County Supervisors to withhold a bridge permit unless the company agreed to extend to 58th St. and Laurel Hill Blvd. At this point the company decided not to extend to Calvary under these conditions.

Seasonal operations on the old Grand St. & Newtown Railroad were both picturesque and physically taxing. Generally in April and occasionally as early as March, open cars were put on the streets: these were stored at both the Meeker Ave. and Newtown barns. By the third week in September the open cars were withdrawn, and the company settled down to prepare for its annual battle with winter. To fight against this formidable adversary, the company had only three effective pieces of equipment: two snow plows, and a sweeper.

The yearly growth in traffic was so encouraging that the company was disposed to increase its rolling stock. At the beginning of the decade, they had 41 cars; as an experiment the company decided in 1882 to purchase six one-horse "jiggers" for the lighter winter traffic. The introduction of these cars raised a storm of protest. They were condemned as a danger to life and property; this was true to some extent. The driver had to eat his meals on the platform while driving, or tie the reins to the platform and go inside the car and eat, leaving the team to proceed without guidance or control. He also had the responsibility of looking out for patrons, the cash box, keeping boys off the rear platform and directing the horses. During the first months of operation several accidents occurred. The use of the cars came to an abrupt end in January 1883 when Mayor Law signed an ordinance passed by the Brooklyn Aldermen requiring all street cars to have a driver and a conductor.

The swelling summer traffic made the few open cars that the company owned inadequate, and in 1883 new cars were added, increasing the fleet to 60. Again in the spring of 1884, seven new open cars were acquired. J. G. Brill Co. delivered five more cars in 1885, and four more in 1889.

The most enduring improvement on the Grand St. R. R. during the 80's was the construction of the Maspeth Depot, an installation that was destined to last through the whole era of trolley operation. The Newtown stables, built in 1876, became inadequate very quickly as the volume of traffic on the Queens County route exceeded expectations. The superintendent pleaded with the directors for more room to grow and his request was granted. The delivery of fresh rolling stock had so strained the capacity of the old depot that as many as a dozen cars at a time had to be parked in the street regularly. The line-up naturally attracted attention, and there was talk of summonses for obstruction and maintaining a nuisance.

On April 2, 1883 work began on the enlargement of the depot, creating accommodation for 50 additional horses and storage for all the cars, including the opens, which had hitherto been stored regularly at Calvary Depot. A new stable was added in the rear for the horses. The new building opened on May 1, and the company immediately installed 30 horses and several of the new open cars.

The summer traffic of 1883-84 quickly demonstrated that even these enlarged facilities were inadequate, so Peter Wyckoff, a director and a son of an ex-president, sold the company a large plot of ground on the south side of Grand St. between Fisk Ave. (now 69th Pl.) and Juniper Ave. The new plot was more than three times the size of the Newtown stables. On the morning of April 9th ground was broken for the new depot at the Juniper Ave. corner. By the first week of May, the framework of the new stables was up; by mid-June the company had moved in with all its equipment.

# Maspeth Depot

*Left*: Maspeth Carbarn 1907, Pay Car No. 9901 on left. Built 1885 by the Grand St. & Newtown R.R., used until December 1908. *Edward Watson collection.*
*Below Left*: Depot work crew poses for a photo, date unknown. *Vincent F. Seyfried collection.*
*Below*: Rear of depot in 1939 with service car No 9640 in the yard. *George Eggers photo/ Vincent F. Seyfried collection.*

The building was then 200 ft. deep with a frontage on Grand St. of 143 ft.; it had stalls for 168 horses with very advanced sanitary arrangements. The roof was largely of skylights, admitting plenty of light and air. In the rear were blacksmith's shops and a large room where the horses were hitched up, occasions requiring at times as many as 15 teams to be kept continually in harness. A third large room was for extras and men off duty and was comfortably furnished. The car house had nine tracks, and room for 75 cars; four tracks led into the building from the street, two turning toward Williamsburgh and two toward Newtown. At the Juniper Ave. corner was a large waiting room for passengers. In the rear of the car house was a transfer table, at that time a very modern innovation. On the second floor were the offices of the superintendent and president.

The old Newtown depot was abandoned by the road; even the waiting room for the Newtown passengers was closed. The papers commented on the closed doors and shutters and that it was all conducive to "thoughts of the deepest melancholy, if not absolute suicide". The saloons felt the loss of patronage severely. In September the stables were up for sale, but the matter could not have been pressed, since the site remained in BRT possession until 1925.

The opening of the Maspeth Depot made a considerable difference in schedules and service. Newtown ceased all at once to be a terminus, and complained at the loss of status. Through operation between the Williamsburgh Ferries and Newtown Village (Elmhurst) ceased, and all the cars now halted at Maspeth with only a shuttle going on to Newtown.

Conductors on Grand St. tended to charge 5 cents for any distance on the shuttle for any ride, and 5 cents on the line west of Maspeth; this meant that anyone from Newtown visiting friends in another Queens County village had to pay 10 cents, a violation of the old fare structure which set a 5 cent limit on any ride in Queens County.

Hardly less interesting among the many changes wrought during the 80's was the gradual liberalization of the fare structure, evolving gradually towards the later 5 cent fare. All during the 70's the company tariffs had remained fairly stable:

5 cents from the ferries to Calvary Cemetery
5 cents from the ferries to Newtown Creek
6 cents from Newtown Creek to Newtown Village (Elmhurst)
3 cents between Fisk Ave. Maspeth (69th Pl.) to Newtown Village

At the very beginning of the 80's there was an agitation in Newtown and Maspeth for lower fares within Queens County. The Fisk Ave. zone point was always a sore spot because Maspeth village lay just beyond, and one had to alight three blocks short of the center of the village to stay within the 3 cent fare; riding into town would have cost 6 cents. The company earned itself some bad publicity besides by refusing to honor its own 5 cent tickets within Queens County on the ground that they were intended for travel within the Brooklyn city limits exclusively.

Just a year and a month later - May 1882 - the horse railroad company pleasantly surprised everyone by scattering circulars announcing a general reduction in fares, and a change of zone points. The fare limit was moved five blocks east to Mazeau St. (72nd Pl.) and charges were as follows:

5 cents from the ferries to Mazeau St., Maspeth
5 cents Mazeau St., Maspeth to Newtown Village

The new arrangement was a great benefit to Brooklyn passengers riding east, the fare was reduced from 11 cents to 5 cents. Maspeth residents going to the city benefited by a reduction from 8 to 5 cents. Newtown, however, gained the least, for a ride to the city was only 1 cent cheaper, 11 to 10 cents, and a ride to Maspeth actually cost more than before, 5 cents instead of 3 cents. Since Mazeau St. was less than a mile away from Newtown village, it would be a considerable saving to walk the final mile and save 5 cents, in other words, the new zone was highly disproportionate: 5 miles for 5 cents, but less than 1 mile, for an additional 5 cents.

Three years later there was a demand for a 5 cent fare for a through ride. By that time the road was averaging 7,668 passengers a day! The inbound fare from Newtown village to the city was slightly modified, too, in the face of rising criticism; a Newtown resident was permitted to ride from the village all the way to Newtown Creek for 5 cents and not merely to Mazeau St.

The subject of transfers from line to line provoked considerable criticism all during the 80's. The Grand St. & Newtown R.R. operated only two lines, the main one to Newtown and the branch to Calvary Cemetery. These two joined at Humboldt & Grand Sts. but the company never permitted passengers coming from the Newtown end of the line to transfer over to the Calvary Cemetery car.

Just as the increased traffic to Newtown and Maspeth gradually forced an increase in rolling stock and the building of an additional car house, so also did the Calvary Cemetery and Greenpoint traffic make desirable an expansion of the Calvary Depot facilities. In August 1889 the line awarded a contract for a new car house and repair shop; the building was a two-story structure at Meeker & Monitor Sts. At the same time four new closed cars were ordered from the Lewis & Fowler Car Co., they arrived in the fall, the last car order from the old Grand Street company.

It was in the 80's that the use of mechanical indicators was first introduced for keeping count of fares paid. In April 1881 the new clocks were mounted in the cars, and passengers were intrigued by the rods and bell pulls manipulated by the conductor. After May 1, 1881 all cars used the new clocks, which were mistaken by passengers for time pieces.

In 1884, we get the first hint of a uniform for operating employees of the road; in July of that year the company issued "a new helmet hat of a neat design" to the men. It took four years to produce any further gesture toward insignia; in the last days of 1888 the drivers were issued conspicuous metal badges to wear on their coats inscribed: "Grand Street and Newtown Railroad Co."

It was in the mid-80's that the sporadic discontent of drivers and conductors with the long hours and hard conditions of the street railroads first crystalized into mass expression. The Grand St. R.R. was no better or worse than most. It was in New York that the first undercurrent of grievance first flamed into open and violent rebellion. For some years the men had worked a 14 hour day for $2.00 pay, in wind and weather, with no job security or benefits. Failing to secure a sympathetic hearing from the directors of the companies, the employees of the Third Ave. and Dry Dock corporations went on strike in March 1886. Cars were stoned in the streets and overturned and the tracks were tampered with. After a month of violence the employees of almost all other horse car railroads joined the strike and completely tied up the street railway system of Manhattan. Faced with such determined demands for shorter hours and more humane conditions, the companies at last yielded, and a new wage pattern of 12 hours work for $2.00 was established. While there were no strikes in Brooklyn, the progress of the struggle was closely watched by both labor and management, and the Brooklyn companies decided very wisely to grant the same terms won by the New York strikers to their employees rather than risk a showdown.

As early as February 1886 President Joost of the Grand St. R.R. attempted to head off potential trouble by voluntarily reducing the hours of employment of drivers and conductors to 11-1/2 hours for the same $2.00 pay. This wise move probably saved the road from labor trouble, for the employees had already largely enrolled in the ranks of the Empire Protective Association, a pioneer operator's union. In April 1886 the company and the union signed an agreement which provided that the working time would, in the future, be 12 hours, or as near that time as possible, for $2.00 a day. The trippers were to receive $1.50; the stablemen $2.25 for 12 hours work, and the horseshoers $3.25 for 10 hours work a day. As some of the trippers hardly paid, they abolished as many as possible, running the regular cars on longer headway. The horses that were fed four times a day would in the future get three meals a day only, as the stableman's day would run from 9 a.m. to 5 p.m..

Morale was high amongst the operating employees as company officials were benevolent and the men were treated with a consideration that speaks well for 19th century labor relations. On occasion the president and directors could be commendably generous; at Christmas of 1888, for example, the men were all paid in advance so as to provide them with funds for enjoyment of the holiday, and in addition every driver, conductor, hostler, stable employee and tow boy received a $2.50 gold piece. Considering that there were over 200 men on the payroll, the extent of the company's generosity can be appreciated. A local resident of Maspeth, a Mr. John Maurice, had begun the custom some years back of presenting each driver and conductor on the Newtown line with $2 at Christmas. When the holiday season of 1889 arrived, the last Christmas under old management, Pres. Wyckoff and Mr. Maurice again extended themselves handsomely. On the whole, therefore, the Grand St. men were well off and the harmonious relationship that prevailed between employers and employees becomes understandable.

Such is the many-sided picture of the little horse railroad as it was in the 80's just before absorption. The process of unification of the various street railroads in Brooklyn had begun in 1888 with the lease of the Bushwick R. R. by the great Brooklyn City system. The Grand St. & Newtown R. R. was an attractive property and could hardly fail to attract the notice of the Brooklyn City R. R. By 1888 it was the ninth largest company in Brooklyn in the number of passengers carried. It came as no surprise, therefore, that the Brooklyn City should make overtures to the directors to add so profitable an operation to its own expanding system. On August 1, 1889 the Brooklyn City R. R. leased the Grand St. R. R. with option to purchase, as soon as the necessary financial settlements with relation to the outstanding stocks and bonds could be completed. By April 1, 1890, almost a year later, plans had been so far perfected that an announcement of purchase appeared in the press, and the road was scheduled to change hands on May 1st. On April 16, the Board of Directors ratified the sale, and on April 28th the stockholders; at 12:01 a.m. on the morning of May 1, 1890 the Brooklyn City R. R. formally took possession. A new age in street railway history was about to unfold. The day of the small plodding "horse railroad" was over, and a new era of unification and electrification was to transform the face of the industry.

# METROPOLITAN AVENUE

The thoroughfare that we know today as Metropolitan Ave. is one of the oldest streets in Brooklyn. It was one of the few streets laid out at the time that the original city of Williamsburgh was founded in 1802; then known as Bushwick St., the name was later changed to Woodhull St. After Grand St. became the "main" street of Williamsburgh in the 1830's and 40's, the streets north and south of it were numbered, and Woodhull St. being two blocks above, was renamed North Second St. The original settlement was at the ferry, and what few houses there were in those days were clustered along what is now Kent Ave. and the handful of streets leading inland. Because of the excellent pasture available for cows and goats in the small marshes along Newtown Creek, a path was worn very early from the settlement along the East River inland to the creek near the hamlet of Bushwick. This crooked, irregular cow path is the origin of todays Metropolitan Ave.

Although the road was very uneven and full of elevations and depressions, it rapidly became the business street of Williamsburgh because it alone gave access to the village of Queens on the farther side of Newtown Creek. The road was officially opened in 1831, and in 1832 the Williamsburgh contractor William Lake received a contract to pave the street. The Bushwick farmers who had large farms in the rich bottom lands along the creek regularly used No. 2nd St. to haul their vegetables to the New York Ferry.

The ferry at the foot of the street was the first to be established in Williamsburgh, and the third on the Long Island side of the river to be opened; only Fulton Ferry and the Catharine St. ferry downtown were older. The earliest commercial establishments along No. 2nd St. were those that catered to the farmers from Bushwick and inland Long Island. These men often drove their teams as far as the ferry and then put up for the night at one of the many hotels, inns and taverns that catered to transients. Of these the old North American Hotel near Driggs Ave., built in 1814, was the most important.

After one left the ferry, the most important spot was that known as the Crossroads, the present intersection of Metropolitan, Bushwick and Maspeth Avenues. At this point two busy turnpike roads from Queens County ended and channeled their heavy wagon traffic into No. 2nd St.

Maspeth Avenue was the roadbed of the Maspeth Ave. & Toll Bridge Co. and led across Newtown Creek into Maspeth, where it ended. Far more important was the Williamsburgh and Jamaica Turnpike, the present Metropolitan Ave. This toll road was one of the earliest on Long Island. Begun in 1814, it was completed in September 1816. The turnpike was a brand new road, not occupying the bed of any pre-existing streets. A glance at the map today will reveal that few streets traverse Brooklyn and Queens in so direct a line; only Myrtle Ave. rivals Metropolitan in directness of alignment. The turnpike crossed Newtown Creek at a point only a few feet south of a grist mill first erected in 1664 by a Dutch settler. In 1816 when the turnpike was opened, the mill was still being operated by two brothers, Stephen and Samuel Masters; they became the first toll keepers. They held the post under lease for about 20 years, and the first toll gate was erected on the turnpike beside their mill. Later, when another toll road, the Brooklyn and Newtown Turnpike (now Flushing Ave.) opened and intersected Metropolitan Ave., the tollgate was moved to the junction of the two toll roads. The original toll gate house on Metropolitan near Morgan Ave. lasted until September 3, `1872, when it was destroyed by fire.

In 1858 the City of Brooklyn first applied the name "Metropolitan Ave." to that part of the turnpike between Bushwick Ave. and Newtown Creek.

The enormous increase in population in Williamsburgh following the Civil War made regular, reliable transportation along the line of No. 2nd St. and Metropolitan Ave. a necessity. The stages were not the answer, their capacity was too small and the primitive paving made fast travel impossible. The fares were high, varying from 6 to 25 cents and the ride could not compare with the smoothness of rail travel. The success of the early horse car lines in Manhattan and the neighboring Grand St. line made the opening of a horse car railroad on No. 2nd St. seem a desirable investment. Not only was it an important business street, but it had the advantage over Grand St. in that it extended beyond Bushwick Ave. into Queens County and the many cemeteries there.

On December 3, 1863 a group of local business men incorporated the "Metropolitan R.R. Co." for a period of 99 years, and with a capital stock of $200,000. The route was somewhat vague: "from a point in the village of Canarsie to a point in the village of Maspeth." Three weeks later the Brooklyn Common Council granted a franchise for the construction of a horse railroad.

The initial construction was paid for in 1865 by executing a mortgage to a Mr. William Peet for $80,000. In 1867 a second mortgage was obtained from Mr. Charles Randall for $75,000 in order to complete the work.

On Monday, September 3, 1866, the company commenced running its cars. The Brooklyn City tracks were used along Kent Ave. from So. 8th St. to No. 1st St. to Wythe Ave., then up Wythe to No. 2nd to Bushwick Ave. The cars of the new company were characterized as "small but rather neat looking."

Before the company could take advantage of the Legislature's permission to extend into Queens County and on to the Lutheran Cemetery, it was first necessary to negotiate with the owners of the Williamsburgh & Jamaica Turnpike, who owned Metropolitan Ave. from the Crossroads eastward to Jamica. On April 15, 1867 the new company obtained from the turnpike officials the right to construct a single track railroad with all necessary turnouts and switches for the three mile stretch from Bushwick Ave. to the Lutheran Cemetery gate at Juniper Ave. The line was constructed and ready for service by October 1, 1867.

The annual income was only about $35,000 so the little company soon went into receivership in 1869. The competition of the Grand St. line was a potent factor in the bankruptcy; the Grand St. line at this early date was already attracting a million and a quarter passengers; the best No. 2nd St. could do was just under half a million. In the spring of 1869 the company's property was sold to one of its directors, Austin Myers, president of the Mechanics National Bank of Syracuse, N.Y.. Myers reorganized the company and incorporated it on June 3, 1869 as the Grand St. Ferry & Middle Village R.R.

The new company and its organization was, for some reason, unsatisfactory to the courts, who decreed that all the properties and franchises of the old Metropolitan R.R. be sold at auction, as the result of foreclosure on the original two mortgages.

The sale took place on April 2, 1870, and by agreement of the trustees the railroad was sold as two parcels. Parcel One covered all that portion of the company's route covered by the Peet mortgage: from Broadway Ferry to Bushwick Ave along with the stable, horses and cars, and the "station", the turnout terminal at Broadway. John Elwell & William Green, directors of the old Metropolitan R.R. cast the winning bid of $40,000. Parcel Two covered that portion of the company's route named in the Randall mortgage: from Metropolitan & Bushwick Avenues eastward to the Lutheran Cemetery. This was bid in for $9,000 by Austin Myers.

On May 24, 1870, the court transferred Parcel One to Elwell & Green, this was the only valuable portion of the original property, for the Queens section originated neither traffic nor revenue. They operated the railroad all during the summer as the Grand St. Ferry & Middle Village R.R. On October 10th, they incorporated the road under the new name, North Second Street & Middle Village R.R. One week later on October 17th they formally transferred their holdings to the new company.

Austin Myers, the successful bidder for Parcel Two, was saddled with a railroad that was inoperable; all the cars, horses and maintenance equipment had been sold to Elwell & Green. Even if he had the equipment, the sparsely settled turnpike would produce infinitesimal revenue; he therefore did the only thing possible under the circumstances: sale of his road to the only rival line that could make use of it, the Grand St. & Newtown R.R. The Grand St. officials were willing to buy and operate the branch line which carried their rail head beyond the Bushwick Ave. terminus; they paid Myers $20,000 for the property.

During the foreclosure proceedings of 1869, a new horse car railroad had appeared on the scene, the Brooklyn & Winfield Ry. Co., whose charter route exactly paralled the Metropolitan Company's line and also the Grand St. & Newtown's main line via Grand and Meeker Avenues to Penny Bridge. This new rival reorganized on May 3, 1870 as the Brooklyn, Winfield & Newtown Ry. Co.: its franchise stated that whenever it was found that any track had already been laid upon any portion of its route, compensation would have to be paid; also, that it might consolidate with such companies. Since tracks were already laid and cars operating on practically its entire route, it would be virtually an intruder on old established lines.

Messrs. Elwell and Green, purchasers of the No. 2nd St. route, were the first to meet the threat. Sometime in 1870 they leased the Brooklyn, Winfield & Newtown Ry. for 95 years, and converted the rights, franchises and privileges for all their unconstructed routes to their North Second St. & Middle Village R.R. in return for $30,000 of the capitol stock of the No. Second St. R.R.

The foreclosure sale of the old Metropolitan R.R. in 1869 had a confusing sequel. Elwell & Green, purchasers of the Peet mortgage covering the western half of the old line, received a deed with a clerical error; the deed included not only their property, but a portion of the Randall mortgage property sold through Myers to the Grand St. road. When the Grand St. line began operating their own branch on July 4, 1870, Elwell & Green objected on grounds that the section of the line from Bushwick Ave. to the creek was named in their mortgage. A lawsuit ensued, and the Grand St. vindicated its operation in the courts. Elwell & Green were forced to retreat, but shortly thereafter, conceived of a clever stratagem to run a rival service to the Lutheran Cemetery in competition with the Grand St. Co.

In July 1870 they made an agreement with their subsidiary, the Brooklyn, Winfield & Newtown Ry., whose franchise included permission to construct along Metropolitan Ave, to Middle Village, to operate cars on their franchise to the cemetery, but over the old tracks laid by the former Metropolitan R.R. on the south side of the road. The Grand St. Co., as the result of litigation, had built its tracks to the cemetery on the north side of the road and operated over them. On October 26, 1870, Messrs. Elwell & Green began running their No. 2nd St. & Middle Village cars to the cemetery in competition with the Grand St. company. Thus two companies were operating the same route, one on either side of the street.

The competition was intense. The Grand St. company in March 1872 made a special purchase of one-horse cars to be run at intervals with the two-horse cars with the view to increasing accommodations to the Lutheran Cemetery. The No. 2nd St. management, not to be outdone, placed in service on March 10th four new 18 ft. cars, capable of seating 24. The previous fall each company had charged 10 cents and both lines ran transfer car shuttles between Newtown Creek and the cemetery. Then just before winter set in, the No. 2nd St. line put on three cars and the Grand St. line countered by cutting the fare to 5 cents. The No. 2nd St. company met this cut and went one better by putting stoves in all the cars, a maneuver that the Grand St. company took three days of hasty carpentry to duplicate. Of course the traveling public was delighted at the spectacle of two companies outdoing each other to court their favor, and luxuriated in the unusually high standard of comfort and service.

As was to be expected, this joint operation could hardly return a profit to both parties. On April 4, 1873 the Grand St. & Newtown R.R. sold their interest in the route back to Myers, who transfered it to the No. 2nd St. company of Elwell & Green. What became of the other tracks is uncertain; either they were tornup or more probably used as the second track for a double track line.

The Broadway Ferry was the nerve center of the company. Here stood at all hours the little 16 ft. horse cars, identified by their green paint scheme and red light at night. In October 1874 a dispute arose between the No. 2nd St. company and the city of Brooklyn over the portion of the farmer's terminal track at the ferry. The city was then in the course of widening, regrading and paving Kent Ave. When workers began tearing up the old pavement, they removed the No. 2nd St. company's old terminus 100 ft. south of Broadway on Kent Ave. which had been in use since 1866. The company then began construction on a new turnout terminus on the northwest corner of Kent Ave. and Broadway. When the companies' intentions were realized by local property owners and politicians to move the terminus north to a point opposite their property, they obtained a temporary injunction against the move. On October 20th a hearing was held; and it was suggested that the company move 75 ft. up from the northeast corner of Kent Ave. and Broadway away from the congested intersection, but the company refused on grounds that it would kill the road. In March 1875 the court denied continuance of the injunction against the new turnout, supporting the company in its contention that the siding constituted a main track, and was authorized by the language of the franchise.

So far as can be ascertained, the No. 2nd St. company used the standard 16 ft. body horse cars of the day. These were painted green, and carried a red light at night to identify them.

The fare structure fluctuated over the years; from opening day to May 1, 1867 through passengers paid 5 cents and way passengers 6 cents. After this date all paid 6 cents, though one could buy twenty 5 cent tickets for $1. The high and uneven fare of 6 cents on the horse car lines during and just after the Civil War was occasioned by the Federal tax of 1/8 cent per passenger levied in 1863 to meet war expenses. The street railroads protested that there was no way of collecting 1/8 cent and they succeeded in persuading Congress to permit them to collect an additional cent and pocket everything over and above the tax. In the spring of 1869 the two houses of Congress finally repealed the War Tax on fares; finally on Oct. 1, 1870 the No. 2nd St. company reduced the rate to 5 cents. At the same time tickets were cut to 4 1/2 cents for adults and 3 cents for children. After October 1870 when the company began operating in Queens County as well as in Kings, a second fare was charged if one traveled east of the Bushwick Ave. stables. The addition of this second fare zone produced bitter complaints from the patrons who lived at or near the line and used the cars. If a passenger took a car at Bushwick Ave. and rode into Maspeth, 10 cents was exacted, though the distance traveled was but 3/4 mile. Refusal in those hardy days meant instant ejection from the car; the day of argument and lawsuits had not yet arrived. The company appears to have been in no hurry to compromise, preferring to stand on its legal rights. The newspapers pointed out that foot

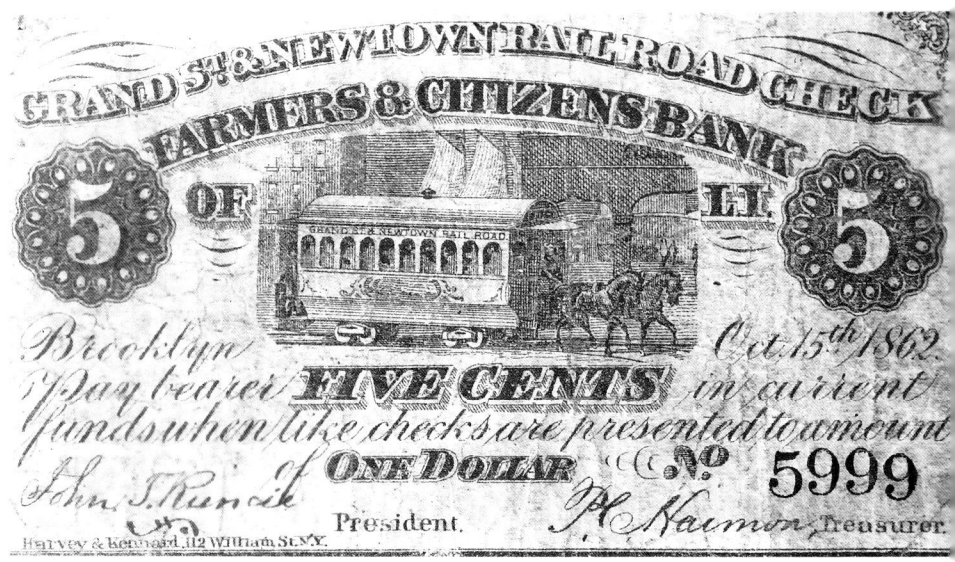

Grand St. & Newtown R.R. ticket, 1862-1867. *Vincent F. Seyfried collection.*

18

travelers on Metropolitan Ave. began to be more numerous than ever before and predicted that they would increase unless the company reconsidered.

When the Grand St. line opened its branch to Newtown in August 1976, the dire predictions of the newspapers seem to have been at least partly fulfilled. A drop in patronage on the outer end of the line in Queens must have taken place, for in October 1878 "bob-tail" cars were put in service. These cars were smaller than the regular cars, with but five windows to a side instead of 6 or 7, and were drawn with one horse instead of a team. They also were one-man operated, a conductor being dispensed with.

It is probably no exaggeration to say that three quarters of the traffic on the Queens end of the Metropolitan Ave. line was cemetery traffic. Interments in the Lutheran Cemetery increased with each passing year, as one would expect considering the nearly solidly German character of Williamsburgh. As the population increased, so did the death rate, and for each person interred, a steady succession of visitors to the grave was assured for a period of several years. All day long during the week the funeral corteges rolled in double and sometimes triple columns along Metropolitan Ave. with scarcely a break on the five miles of road between the ferries and the cemetery gates.

Pfingst Monday was a favorite Lutheran occasion for visiting the dead and hosts of people from Brooklyn and New York thronged the highway. Today the custom of making a visit to the cemetery a family outing has died out through competition with other and more attractive outdoor amusements, but in our grandfather's day before the auto made traveling afar possible, a Sunday outing to the cemetery was highly thought of. Whole families flocked to the cars and rode out to the suburbs, where mother and the children planted flowers and tended the grass, while father dropped into one of the many hostelries along Metropolitan Ave. for his pint of beer. Often the whole family partook of a picnic lunch at the grave or on a nearby lawn before taking the car back to the city.

During the period 1875-80 there was a strong movement in New York and Philadelphia to get away from horse operation and to adapt steam to street railway traffic, and for several years it became the vogue to experiment with "steam cars" or "dummies" as they were called. In Philadelphia about a dozen such cars operated with some success and the report of this trial prompted several New York companies to experiment with steam cars. The 2nd Ave., 3rd Ave., and Bleecker St. lines tried the method in New York, and in Brooklyn the Broadway R.R., Bushwick R.R. and Brooklyn City R.R. all gave the idea a trial on their suburban routes. On April 12, 1877 the North Second St. &

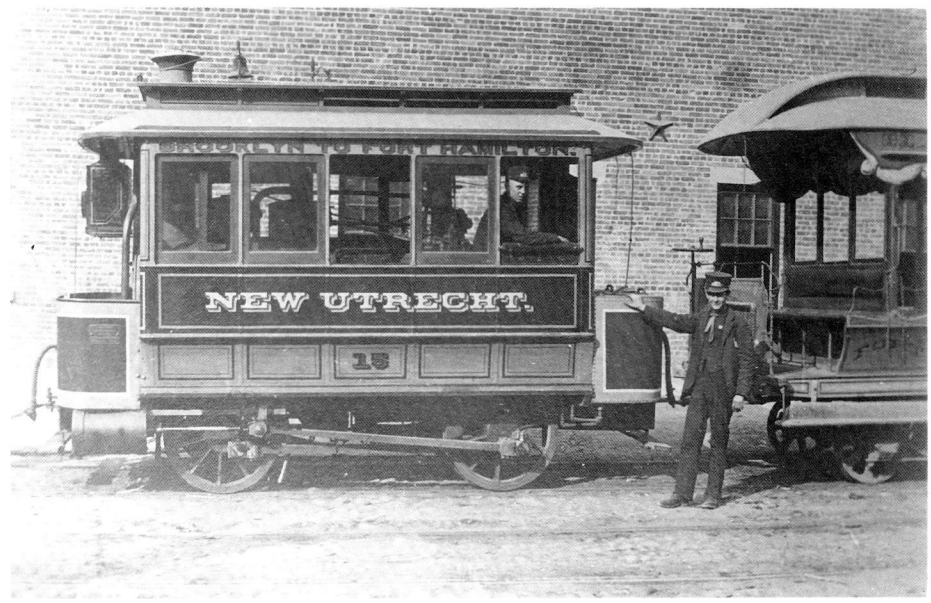
Steam dummy No 15 with coach trailer. *Vincent F. Seyfried collection.*

Middle Village R.R. applied to the Board of Supervisors of Newtown to make a trial of the improved steam car on Metropolitan Ave. Nothing seems to have come of the project so far as is known, but it is interesting to note that the management was at least forward-looking enough to consider such an experiment.

The years 1879 and 1880 brought an important and permanent stimulus to business and rail travel along Metropolitan Ave.: the opening of St. John's Cemetery. A large portion of the road's revenue came from the Lutheran Cemetery traffic; this time the Catholic Church provided a new source of revenue.

The Metropolitan Ave. horse car line probably would have continued on its sleepy, drowsy way for several more years had it not been rudely jarred into alertness by the appearance on its own territory of a new and completely unexpected intruder, the Bushwick R.R. Co. When St. John's Cemetery opened in 1880, the old horse railroad had been delighted because it alone came anywhere near the cemetery gates. However, others had been eyeing this development from afar and resolved to profit by it.

The Bushwick R.R. had opened a line along So. 4th St., Meserole, Bushwick Ave. to Myrtle Ave. on June 1 1868. In the 70's two other lines had been opened, one on Tompkins Ave. and another on Graham Ave., Driggs, Manhattan and Greenpoint Avenues to the Greenpoint Ferry. In 1878 the company had surprised everyone by opening a steam dummy line along Myrtle and Cypress Avenues to the Cypress Hills Cemetery. Because the new cemetery route proved so profitable, the officials resolved to tap the Lutheran and St. John's cemetery traffic as well.

In December 1880 the Bushwick R.R. purchased space on the south side of Metropolitan Ave., the site of the present Myrtle Ave. elevated terminus, and in August 1881 the depot was completed. There were no roads from the city line to the cemetery, so a private right-of-way had to be purchased from the farmers. On September 1, 1881 the new dummy line opened, and because it was fast and highly novel, it attracted much of the cemetery business and cut deeply into the revenues of the N. 2nd St. horse car road.

The Bushwick steam dummy route was competition of the most formidable kind, for the poor No. 2nd Ave. road. The old company provided a ride at 5 m.p.h. on generally poor track in horse cars that were old, creaky and poorly maintained; the Bushwick R.R. offered a ride to the same destination in steam-coach cars offering Pullman like comfort over a newly-ballasted roadbed and at speeds of 10-12 m.p.h., and for the same fare: 8 cents. In addition the dummies had the advantage of novelty and capacity; they accomadated 22 persons and more in an attached trailer.

Faced with such a rival the No. 2nd St. had but two alternatives: give up and lose their investment, or improve their plant to meet the competition. In August 1881 the company advertised an excursion fare ticket to attract business. For 55 cents the ticket offered a ride in the company's cars from the ferries out to Fresh Pond station, where the purchaser could transfer to trains for Rockaway.

To overcome this overwhelming threat to the company's solvency, the No. 2nd St. company decided to out-do its rival, and build an extension right up to the gates of St. John's Cemetery. The privilege of exclusive access to the Lutheran Cemetery could never again be recovered, but by building eastward along Metropolitan Ave., it could gain a monopoly on St. John's Cemetery traffic. Accordingly on September 3, 1881 the company, without notice of its intentions, commenced carting ties and rails along Metropolitan Ave. for building the new extension. Meanwhile, horse car accommodations were increased along the avenue to attract business from the dummy but without much success.

During the fall months the ties were laid and the rail put down on the new single track extension. The Newtown Highway Commission had become aware of the extension and was angry at the company's failure to seek their permission to trespass on the highway. About January 1st they applied for an injunction to stop the work. The argument came up before the Brooklyn Supreme Court on the 16th; the newspapers took the company's part, and saw the extension not a violation of law, but an improvement too valuable to oppose. The court dismissed the injunction on the technicality that the legal title of the company had not been fully and properly set forth in the application. By this time the ice and snow of winter had effectively interrupted the track laying.

With the coming of spring the company, instead of running its cars to the end of track to attract customers, set up a foolish and short-sighted arrangement that alienated passengers. For the first decade the company operated to Middle Village, it had terminated at Juniper Ave. John Sutter, the marble yard owner, had induced the company to extend the track 800 ft. eastward to the entrance to the southern half of the Lutheran Cemetery, and had subscribed a large portion of the expense. The company then operated over this short segment. With the opening of the cemetery visiting season in 1881, the company suddenly cut back its cars to Juniper Ave. again, and installed a one-horse shuttle car on the extension, for a ride on which a 2 cent additional fare was charged. This gouge was irritating enough, but the company added insult to injury by declining to run the the shuttle on some Sundays forcing the passengers to walk.

In the light of such fumbling, it is hardly wondered why the No. 2nd St. company was so disliked by its patrons; the regular accommodations were poor enough to irritate the villagers, but this earned the illwill of visitors as well. By the 3rd week of June the new extension to Dry Harbor Rd. (80th St.) at the gates of St. John's Cemetery was completed. The last spike, reputedly of silver, was driven by Town Assessor Closius, who lived on the corner. Although the population were grateful for the increased facilities to Middle Village, they found it hard to forgive the company the extra 2 cents charged on the shuttle.

In January 1884 the company took pity on its benumbed patrons and installed stoves on the cars for the first time since the opening of the extension. With the approach of summer a fresh source of competition appeared in the form of the LIRR. The Manhattan Beach division instituted rapid transit between Long Island City and East New York with trains stopping at Fresh Pond station (Metropolitan Ave,). Riders who had hitherto crossed to Brooklyn on ferries and taken the No. 2nd St. cars to the cemeteries now rode out to Middle Village and paid only 2 cents to the horse car company instead of 8 cents.

The whole road over the five year period 1880-85 showed a slight decline in revenues even with the opening of St. John's Cemetery and the great increase in travel thereto. Too much patronage was being lost to the dummy competitor and to the railroad. The insensitivity on the part of the company to the wishes of the people, and the indifferent running of the cars contributed to the declining financial picture, so it is not suprising that the road failed to earn the interest on its obligations. Accordingly, on August 9, 1884 the road was thrown into receivership, and Richard H. Greene, the president, was appointed receiver. On November 11, 1884 the line was sold by court order and knocked down to the trustees of the mortgage, James Elwell and William Green. The mortgage had been contracted May 1, 1875 and these men had been designated trustees; the former had brought suit for foreclosure because of non-payment of interest. The result was that the North Second St. & Middle Village R.R. passed out of existance, and on February 11, 1885 the road was reorganized as the Brooklyn, Buskwick & Queens County R.R.

The road had become so run-down since 1870 that immediate efforts at rehabilitation were made. One of the most important improvements undertaken in years was the building of a new depot. Since 1866 the company had housed its cars, horses and offices in two or three ramshackle old sheds at Bushwick and Metropolitan Avenues. The site selected for the new depot was a vacant stretch of land on the south side of Metropolitan Ave. between Onderdonk and Woodward Avenues just inside the Queens County line. According to BRT records this plot had been purchased in 1882. We do not know just what buildings were erected on the site, but they housed offices for the dispatcher and the receiver of moneys, and space for all the cars of the company. The work on the new depot began sometime in September 1884 and was completed in mid-November. At the same time part of the line received new rails.

One of the only known views of Newtown Docks. Looking south-west twards the canal, July 12, 1918. *Vincent F. Seyfried collection.*

Even more welcome was the appearance of new cars for the first time in over 10 years. In May the first new vehicle appeared in service in Middle Village and created a sensation, the oldest inhabitants gathering in groups and recalling the time "before the war" when a similar event had happened!

At about this time the new drawbridge over Newtown Creek opened. The old bridge had fallen into such disrepair that two temporary wooden structures had been pressed into service. The new bridge was 165 ft. long and 33 ft. wide and turned on a stone pier.
During construction both the Metropolitan and Grand St. car lines had to lay tracks on a temporary bridge with consequent delays. By the end of August 1885 the bridge was finished but neither company had as yet laid track on the approaches. The two company's wrangled over which would have priority in crossing the bridge; also who should pay for the joint tracks on the bridge. Both arguments were amicably compromised after 10 days quarreling. Finally, on December 11, 1885 the bridge opened for travel and the cars once again ran on schedule.

The temporary bridge over Newtown Creek, at the junction of Grand St. & Metropolitan Ave. The sign reads *"Driving over the bridge faster than a walk is forbidden under penalty of law. Cars and vehicles must go slow."* Vincent F. Seyfried collection.

The year 1886 brought a further change of management to the company. On March 3, 1886 the receivership was terminated and the line was bought by the New Williamsburgh & Flatbush R.R. Co. This company had been incorporated in 1866 and in January 1871 opened a north-south line through Brooklyn from the Broadway Ferry through Broadway, Driggs, Division, Lee and Nostrand Avenues to Malbone St. On August 5, 1885 they opened a branch along Lorimer St., Driggs, Manhattan Ave., Meserole Ave., Franklin and Greenpoint Avenues to the Greenpoint Ferry. This latter line intersected the No. 2nd St. line at Lorimer, and connecting curves were laid at that corner to make a physical connection between the two companies.

Under the progressive New Williamsburgh & Flatbush management, the old No. 2nd St. line took a new lease on life. An order for new cars to replace the old rattletraps was given immediatly, and repairs were begun on the track. As early as April, one month after the purchase, new horse cars were placed in service on the No. 2nd St. and Metropolitan Ave. line, and were greatly appreciated by the Middle Village patrons. more new and handsome cars appeared in May, and the headway on weekends was reduced to 3 minutes, an unheard-of accommodation!

The year 1886 was a momentus one for the great street railway companies of New York, for the first great struggles between capital and labor erupted into violence at this time. For years the companies had hired and fired freely, and paid varying wage scales. In March and April 1886 most of New York was tied up by street car strikes, and the repercussions of this struggle were felt in Brooklyn. The New York companies compromised at last on a scale of 12 hours work for $2.00 and this formula was generally adopted all over town.

The employees of the Lee & Nostrand, Greenpoint & Lorimer, and No. 2nd St. lines were not satisfied at first with this settlement, claiming that it would operate less to their benefit than the old 14 hour table, there being at the time not a single straight 12 hour run on the entire table, all carrying them from 18-20 minutes over the promised run, while instead of a half hour for dinner, they would get only 12-14 minutes. The schedule was taken up by the union, the Empire Protective Association and the company, and in the last days of March 1886 settled.

With the end of the 80's the little Metropolitan horse car line was at its best and it seems appropriate at this point to pause and take a close look at the line itself and the neighborhood it served. Equipment and service were at their peak at this time; and until the end the company operated a nicely balanced fleet of 25 open cars and 22 closed cars, all of which were fairly new and well maintained. All the cars ran out of the one depot at Woodward and Onderdonk Avenues; with the whole trip from the ferries to St. John's taking 1 hour and 10 minutes, and only 50 minutes after 1889.

The new management reduced fares after 1886; the fares had been 5 cents from the ferries to Flushing Ave., and 3 cents for any ride east of that in Queens, plus an additional 3 cents on the extension. The new fares were 5 cents for any ride in Brooklyn, and an additional 1 cent for Queens County.

Strangely enough, even though the fares were reduced, riding continued to decline from its height of 1887:

| | | | | | |
|---|---|---|---|---|---|
| 1881 | 1,375,488 | 1885 | – | 1889 | 1,454,808 |
| 1882 | 1,356,069 | 1886 | – | 1890 | – |
| 1883 | 1,351,428 | 1887 | 1,701,500 | 1891 | 1,380,159 |
| 1884 | 1,355,631 | 1888 | 1,527,600 | | |

It is hard to explain, but probably too much profitable Williamsburgh traffic was lost to Grand St., while in Queens the company was too dependent on weekend cemetery patronage, and thus at the mercy of the weather. In winter there was little cemetery traffic, and regular riders of Middle Village too few to support a long suburban line.

In December 1888 the New Williamsburgh & Flatbush decided to pull off the "big cars" on Metropolitan Ave., and substitued 5-window jiggers in their place. These were numbered in the 200 series.

In April 1889 the company started to rebuild the tracks through Middle Village.

An imaginary journey by horse car from the Broadway Ferries will make more vivid than any other method the changing neighborhood and pastoral scenery along the six miles of the company's route. We walk over to the siding at the northwest corner of Kent Ave. and Broadway and board one of the little green cars with the red light for night identification. As we leave the stand and roll up Kent Ave., nearly all the buildings along the river front are sugar refineries, large brick affairs full of boilers and steam vats. At Grand St. we turn off into Water St., go a block, pass the Grand St. Ferry, and turn into North 1st St., continue for a block, and up Wythe to No. 2nd St. This rather roundabout way seems to have been designed on purpose to pick up as many ferry passengers as possible, and to give the company the chance to store a whole string of cars, if it wished, in side streets near the ferries to accommodate the rush when the boats docked.

The horses strain to pull the car up the grade to Driggs Ave.; looking out the window, small stores of all kinds can be seen, tea merchants, umbrella makers, groceries, fire companies, churches, small hotels, breweries, wagon makers and the hundred other occupations that the teaming city supports. At Driggs Ave. we cross the Brooklyn City tracks and run downhill past Roebling, Havemeyer, Marcy and Rodney Sts. The many saloons cater to neighborhood trade and to farmers on their way to market from Bushwick.

Between Rodney St. and Union Ave. the road drops to its lowest point and floods with heavy rain, passengers often having to stand on seats to keep dry. From Union Ave. we climb slowly passing Lorimer, Leonard, Ewen Sts., Graham Ave. and Humboldt St. At Lorimer, we cross the tracks of the Greenpoint & Lorimer line of the New Williamsburgh & Flatbush R.R., and on Graham we cross the Brooklyn City's Flushing Ave. line, and the Bushwick R.R.'s Greenpoint line. At Humboldt St. we rumble over the Cemetery line of the Grand St. R.R.

A block beyond Bushwick Ave. we reach the highest point on No. 2nd St. and pass into Metropolitan Ave. and the sparsely settled 18th Ward. The car goes downhill decending into the meadowlands and swamps bordering Newtown Creek. For a century this has been the stronghold of the Bushwick farmers, as late as 1884 there were still 117 barns in this area housing 1,195 cows! As the 80's wore on, Newtown Creek became polluted from two sources: Greenpoint sewage, and the oil and timber works along the Brooklyn shore of the creek. This made the land unfit for cultivation and it was gradually turned into storage yards and dock facilities. The banks of the creek were gradually bulk-headed and the low areas filled, in the late 80's.

At Newtown Creek the car crosses the new bridge and then traverses a flat, empty area of low marsh lands and occasional houses. About five city blocks beyond the creek we cross the Queens County border and stand before the car depot. From here we begin a slow upward climb and soon cross the Bushwick Branch of the LIRR, and some blocks further, Flushing Ave. Here on the southwest corner is Metropolitan Park, a picnic grove that lasted down to World War I. Here also is the fare zone limit, and the conductor comes around to collect an additional 1 cent (after 1886).

Before us lies the sleepy little hamlet of East Williamsburgh; occasional houses dot the avenue, but settlement is still very thin.

At Fresh Pond Rd. we pass Rommel's new hotel and enter the precincts of Middle Village. At this busy corner is the Fresh Pond station of the railroad, and trains from Long Island City and Bushwick regularly stop here on their way to Jamica and Manhattan Beach. On the southwest corner is an old hotel and saloon (still standing in 1957). As we move into the village proper, we pass a good number of homes and saloons fronting the street. The great expanse of the Lutheran Cemetery looms up on our left, first opened in March 1851. Approaching nearer the village we pass Wendel's Hotel, Sutter's monument yard,

Timmes' Halfway Hotel, and at Juniper Ave., Seib's Central Hotel and Schuhmacher's Hotel and saloon. Between Wendel's and Sutter's property is the new depot of the Bushwick R.R. dummy line running to Ridgewood. Juniper Ave. marked the terminal of the horse car line and is now the end of double track. The driver and conductor get off here and drop into the hotels for refreshment.

Little Middle Village prided itself upon its "extensive marble works, the large cemeteries, the best patronized hotels, several churches, four public schools, a great variety of business and private residences. Schuhmacher's Hotel on the south side of the street opposite Juniper Ave. still survives today as a restaurant; in May 1888, John Sutter, the owner, sold it for $28,000 to John Niederstein of Yorkville, and the old establishment still bears his name today.

Changing to the shuttle that will take us to the end of the line, we board a light five-window car drawn by one horse. The driver runs the car and acts as conductor collecting the 3 cent

Newtown Creek Bridge with a B&QT Peter Witt crossing on the Grand St. line.
*Bill Molnar photo/Bill Meyers collection.*

fare. From Juniper Ave. we move along on single track, and 800 ft. eastward pass the "upper Gate" of Lutheran Cemetery, opening on the south half of that vast tract. A short distance beyond, we move slowly past the Methodist church and the Middle Village Hotel, and a few hundred feet further we come to the end of the line at St. John's Cemetery. The main gate of the cemetery and the horse car terminus are at Dry Harbor Rd. (80th St.) and Metropolitan Ave. On the northwest corner is the new St. John's Hotel opened in October 1885 and familiarly called "Hirsch's Corner" after the owner John Hirsch. We have journeyed 6 miles and the trip has taken one hour and ten minutes.

In the last years of independent ownership and operation there were few innovations on Metroplitan Ave. As early as 1890 electrification was considered by the line. The local citizens became electric conscious when the first poles and wires for electric lighting were set up at Christmas of 1891. Even though electrification was approved by the Town of Newtown, the decline in earnings made it unprofitable to proceed. No interest on the bonds could be paid from the scanty receipts of the road, so on Oct. 29, 1891 the line was again thrown into receivership, Frank Hartshorn, appointed as receiver. Two months later the court ordered the railroad sold, and on May 26, 1892, it was knocked down to John Englis and Henry D. Donnelly for $200,000. It was explained at the time that during the spring, summer and fall the road was well patronized by New Yorkers going to the cemetery and suburban resorts, but in the winter months the traffic was small. The old company had also been put to great expense of late shifting its tracks because of the changing of grade of the streets for paving and the construction of sewers. There were a number of judgements outstanding against the road, totaling $280,000, among others a feed bill for $15,000. The foreclosure action conveniently wiped out all the indebtedness and all obligations to the stockholders. Englis and Donnelly, the purchasers, acted in their capacity as trustees for the bondholders, who now proceeded to reorganize the road for the last time. More than half the bonds were held by the Englis family. The Brooklyn, Bushwick & Queens County R. R. now passed out of existence and on Sept. 10, 1892 the road was reorganized as the Broadway Ferry & Metropolitan Ave. R. R.

In this final year of private operation (1892-93) nothing of note was accomplished. On Dec. 31, 1892 the company filed for an extension of route along Wythe Ave. down to the Broadway Ferry but this was never built. We can surmise from this that Kent Ave. was becoming overcrowded with horse car and wagon traffic to and from the ferries, and the company sought a route of its own to avoid delays and gain maneuverability. In March of 1893 the company again filed for an extension from the corner of Metropolitan and Varick Avenues down Varick to Flushing Ave. This spur, unlike the others, was actually built to give access to a street railroad dump and dock on Newtown Creek between Meserole and Montrose Ave. The B.R.T. property records show that this dock property had been purchased by the Broadway Railroad and access to it could only be gained by a spur off Metropolitan Ave.

In November 1893, months before the end of private operation, the company won the approval of the Common Council for electrification of the line on Metropolitan Ave. and N. 2nd St. Meanwhile the officers of the company had been busy negotiating a sale of the company's property and franchises to a new and wealthy group of financiers, with a view to integrating the Metropolitan Ave. line into a larger street railway network. Certainly, experience had demonstrated three or four times over that the hard fact was that the line could not be made to pay as an independent operation. Accordingly, on Jan. 16, 1894 the road was sold to a new and larger operating company, the Brooklyn, Queens County & Suburban R. R., and its days as a horse car "toonerville" line came to an end.

# THE CORONA, FRESH POND AND FLUSHING AVENUE EXTENSION

With the coming of the 90's vast changes were in store for the street railway systems in Brooklyn. There was a growing tendency in almost every important segment of American industry at that time to merge, consolidate and absorb small individual holdings into combines of unparalleled size and power. The Civil War had furnished the initial impetus for industrial expansion and exploitation of the country's natural resources. The handicraftsman and the small family manufactory became obsolete almost overnight in the face of an unprecedented demand for the many sinews of war: wood, iron, fabrics, explosives, tools, transport, ect. Large new factories grew up, labor flocked to the cities to work in industry, and fortunes were made with unbelievable rapidity. When the war ended, the country could never again return to the leisurely pace and isolation of the 1840's and 1850's. The post-Civil War years saw an immense expansion of the national economy on every side. The frontier was pushed ever westward, new cities grew up, the population doubled and trebled, and an age of expansive prosperity dawned on a scale hitherto unknown in the history of the country. The large fortunes made during the Civil War created a moneyed class made up of shrewd, far-sighted business men who read the signs of the times accurately, and who had the means to carry out the daring schemes they envisaged. These men had learned the power that the combination of money and monopoly could achieve, and they saw that the day of the little man was over. Shrewdly, carefully and often with complete disregard of the moral and ethical issues of their moves, they crushed their competition outright, or progressively strangled them until they were ripe for absorption. The story of the Rockefellers and the Standard Oil Trust, Andrew Carnegie and the U. S. Steel Corp. are but two familiar examples of this Age of Giants in the American scene.

In the field of railroads a similar process was going on. One by one the small roads were either purchased or financially maneuvered into larger and larger units until by the 90's the giant combines like the Pennsylvania, New York Central, Erie, Baltimore & Ohio, New Haven, etc., had taken final form.

It was but natural that this national trend should filter down to the street railways of the day. The first step in this direction in Brooklyn was the organization and incorporation of the Brooklyn Heights R. R. in April 1887. The directors behind this project were all wealthy bankers with vast capital at their disposal. Although their ostensible purpose was the organization of a street railway, the real one was to absorb as many as possible of the small street railway properties in Kings County as could be secured, and to run them as one great system, with control, finance, and policy to be vested in the Brooklyn Heights R. R. In the Brooklyn of 1887 the largest street railway operation in the county was that of the Brooklyn City R. R., which operated about 200 route miles. This was also the original company in Brooklyn, having started in 1854. Over the years the Brooklyn City system had gradually expanded through extension into newly built-up areas like Flatbush and East New York.

It was obvious that the Brooklyn City R. R. was the ideal nucleus around which to build a county-wide system, and the Brooklyn Heights capitalists resolved to secure stock control of that road as their first move. In 1888 this was accomplished and the directors embarked immediately on a program of expansion by purchase. In July 1888 they secured control of their first property, the Bushwick Railroad Co., by leasing it for 999 years. This purchase added 12 miles of routes.

One year later, August 1889, four more properties were leased;
1- The New Williamsburgh & Flatbush R.R. operating the Nostrand Ave. line, and its subsidiary, the Greenpoint & Lorimer St. R.R., operating the Lorimer St. route. These accounted for 6-1/4 route miles.
2-The Grand St. & Newtown R.R., operating the Grand St. line and the Meeker Ave. branch; 8-1/4 route miles.
3-Calvary Cemetery, Greenpoint & Brooklyn, operating lines on Greenpoint Ave., Union Ave. and Throop Ave.; 6 route miles.
4-Brooklyn Crosstown R.R. running along the waterfront from Long Island City to Erie Basin; 5 miles.

On October 30-31, 1890 all these five properties were merged into the Brooklyn City system. Two years later another small line on 39th St. and along 2nd Ave., called the South Brooklyn Street R.R. Co., was added to the growing system. The final step was taken on February 14, 1893 when the entire Brooklyn City R.R. with all its recent purchases, was itself leased to the Brooklyn Heights R.R. for 999 years, with the lease taking effect June 6th.

Under private management passenger traffic on the Grand St. & Newtown R.R. had fluctuated considerably. The Newtown branch was "summer road" in the sense that it carried heavy traffic only from June to September. The most profitable line was still the Calvary or Meeker Ave. line. By integrating cars, stables and employees into a common pool, management hoped to reduce operating costs. In June 1890 the former office and waiting room on Kent Ave. was closed. The car crews received orders the same month to adopt the navy blue uniforms and white cap of the Brooklyn City R.R. Efforts were made immediately to improve service: the Newtown shuttle cars were repainted and refurbished and a midnight car for Williamsburgh was dispatched nightly from Maspeth stables. On the Meeker Ave. line a similar late car was run to the Penny Bridge at 11:45 p.m. The horse stock at Maspeth stables was augmented in September 1890 with the purchase of 40 new horses for the Grand St. service. The Brooklyn City R.R. achieved a reputation for being progressive and attracted immediate favorable comment by sending its agents along Grand St. in December 1890 to gather signatures from the property owners for permission to electrify the line.

Coincident with the laying of new pavement, was the double tracking of the Grand St. line from Newtown Creek to Maspeth stables. By the end of October the double track was complete to the little village of Melvina.

For a whole year work was suspended, only to be resumed in the spring of 1893 as part of a much more ambitious project, namely, building an extension all the way to Bowery Bay or North Beach, the new bathing resort on the sound. On December 19, 1892 the town board of Newtown granted the Brooklyn City R.R. a franchise to build along Corona Ave., Elmhurst, from Broadway to Junction Ave. and along Junction Ave. to Bowery Bay Road, then along that country lane to the beach. The Railroad Commission granted permission for electric operation September 25, 1893.

The first step in the new project was the repairing of the old Newtown stables on Broadway, closed and boarded up since 1885 when the Maspeth stables had opened. Large quantities of rails and ties were being stored at the Maspeth depot, and 900 men were being recruited as a labor force. In March 1893 wagons began to distribute the 80 lb. rail all along the route.

On the morning of April 5, 1893 one hundred men were set to work in Melvina where the double track of the Grand St. line then ended. As the track laying proceeded eastward, the Highway Commission made sure that the company paved between the tracks with granite blocks and not cobblestones. By April 20th the tracks had been completed nearly to Corona. As they approached the crossing of the LIRR on Junction Ave., tension developed almost immediately. How would the LIRR react in the light of its well-known opposition to crossing at grade? During the afternoon of April 18th the prospect of a battle between employees of the LIRR and BCRR arose. A rumor had been spread that the BCRR would attempt to lay the castings necessary to cross the LIRR tracks. To prevent this, the LIRR dispatched several engines to Corona, ready to run back and forth all night to prevent the crossing. The LIRR superintendent, with the backing of deputy sheriffs and other men, was ready for a show of force, but the BCRR shrewdly declined to force a crossing at nite. The following morning the LIRR obtained an injunction from the courts just to be on the safe side.

The prospect of a street railway in Corona touched off a real estate boom in the village. In the last days of May 1893 the railroad dumped loads of iron trolley poles along Corona Ave. By pushing the work even on Sunday, the company drew down on its head the wrath of the Episcopal rector of St. James at the corner of Broadway and Corona Ave. Because the hollow poles fell with such a deafening noise as to disturb the services in church, the priest caused the arrest of the two truck drivers but the company bailed out the men and paid their $5 fine when they were arraigned the following day.

In the last week of June 1893 a crossover was installed in the double tracks in National Ave., Corona, immediately south of the LIRR tracks, thus giving notice to the steam railroad and the people that this was to be the terminus of the trolley line until the extension to Flushing could be arranged.

On July 4, 1893 the Grand St. horse cars began running through to Corona station. From Corona the time to Maspeth was 25 minutes, and to the Grand St. Ferry an hour and five minutes; the fare was 10 cents. Like most new lines the Corona extension was heavily patronized. The Newtown shuttle was extended from the village to service this outermost extension of the system, and began to assume an importance that it had never before enjoyed. Large numbers of residents rode the shuttle car to Maspeth stables, where they changed for the city car which in August 1893 was being operated on a four minute headway.

Even while the Corona extension was being built, construction was proceeding apace on another sector. At the same time the Town of Newtown granted the franchise for Corona Ave. and Junction Ave. to the Brooklyn City R. R., a second franchise had been awarded for the whole length of Fresh Pond Road (Dec. 19, 1892).

Fresh Pond Road is one of the oldest roads in Queens County. It appears to have been laid out in 1680 to give the Newtown people access to the lands near the present cemeteries of Evergreens and Cypress Hills. At that early period it was a narrow lane leading from the New Bushwick Lane (Evergreen Ave.) at about the present Central Ave. and Moffat St. to the "Fresh Ponds" of Newtown. The lane was named for the large ponds near the southeast angle of the road and Mt. Olivet Ave.; most of these ponds survived until the beginning of the building boom in Ridgewood in the late 80's and 90's.

In the first week of May 1893 the tracks were laid along Fresh Pond Road in two sections, for good reason that the LIRR again acted as a barrier at Metropolitan Ave. where the Montauk Branch of the railroad had to be crossed at grade. To avoid conflict the gap over the railroad was left untouched. The northern track section extended from Grand St. to the railroad, and the southern section from the railroad to the Lutheran dummy line tracks of the former Bushwick R. R.

On July 15, 1893 the Brooklyn City wiring gangs made the mistake of attempting to string trolley wires over the Fresh Pond crossing, but they had no sooner got them in place over the railroad track than officers in the employ of the latter company cut them down, and remained on guard to see that no further attempt was made to put them in place. The LIRR claimed that the trolley wires endangered the lives of the brakeman on the freight cars while passing under the wires, but everyone recognized that this was but a pretext to slow down the construction of a potential competitor.

The end of the year 1893 saw the completion of both the Junction Ave. and Fresh Pond lines effectively blocked because of grade crossing difficulties, but a third large project did achieve completion, namely, the opening of Flushing Ave. to a junction with Grand St. in Maspeth. The west end of Flushing Ave. in downtown Brooklyn is now a very old street dating back to colonial days. Old Flushing Ave. began at the Wallabout Mill Pond (now part of the Navy Yard) at about North Elliot Place and ran east to Bushwick Ave. In 1805 it became a toll road called the Brooklyn and Newtown Turnpike. In 1835 the western end was deeded to the City of Brooklyn. In 1850 Flushing Ave. was extended out to Broadway and in 1858 to Bushwick Ave. Beyond Bushwick Ave. the old road ran in a very serpentine fashion, winding both north and south of the present improved avenue. In 1868 the Brooklyn Common Council surveyed a new straightened route eastward as far out as the city line, and hewing as closely as possible to a mean average of the old curves.

The Brooklyn City R. R. began operating along lower Flushing Ave. in 1854. Some time in the 60's operation was extended to

Broadway. On June 24, 1867 the Graham Ave. line was opened, and on Nov. 15, 1867 the Flushing Avenue cars began running up Graham Ave. from the old terminal at Broadway to No. 2nd St. For years and years thereafter this operation remained unchanged. The next stretch of track along Flushing Ave. was that laid by the Bushwick R. R. between Bushwick Ave. and Knickerbocker Ave. in 1886.

Hot on the heels of the pavers were the track gangs of the Brooklyn City R. R. On Oct. 26, 1889 they had obtained from the supervisors and Commissioner of Highways of the Town of Newtown permission to extend a double track along Flushing Ave. from the city line (Onderdonk Ave.) to the Bushwick Tracks of the LIRR. On July 1, 1889 the Brooklyn City R. R. had secured from the Common Council of the City of Brooklyn permission to extend their tracks from the old terminal at Graham Ave. to the Bushwick Railroad's tracks at Bushwick Ave., and from Knickerbocker Ave. to the city Line (Onderdonk Ave.). These two grants of 1889 thus covered all the gaps in the proposed continuous route into Queens County.

In the first week of October 1889 laborers began laying the horse railroad tracks from Onderdonk Ave., then the city line, eastward toward Metropolitan Ave. In December the contractor was at work filling in this stretch of Flushing Ave., after which the Brooklyn City people laid rails and paved between their rails and two feet on either side as required by the franchise. Winter interrupted the progress of the work but grading and paving was resumed in March 1890. In mid-April a force of 75 men was active in laying ties and rails. So favorable was the progress that on Saturday, April 19, 1890, Flushing Ave. horse cars began running into Queens County as far as Metropolitan Ave.

Only the segment from Metropolitan Ave. to the junction with Grand St. in Maspeth remained to be opened. In July 1891 the county awarded damages to the farmers and residents through whose lands the new avenue was laid out. Two years passed and by July of 1893 the extension was so far completed that the road was passable for wagons. Grading was pushed during late July and a start made on paving.

In the first days of August 1893 the Brooklyn City management made preparations to lay tracks on the newly opened avenue. Track gangs went to work about August 15th and worked their way rapidly eastward. Pres. Lewis of the railroad company pleased everyone by announcing that the trolley system would be introduced on the new Flushing Ave. extension on Oct. 7th on a trial basis, and on regular schedule the following day. This optimistic pronouncement proved premature; the electric cars failed to appear and the section lay unused for three years more. A glance at the map quickly reveals the reason: in this short stretch of Flushing Ave. are two crossings of the LIRR, one over the Montauk Branch and one over the Bushwick Branch. The LIRR emphatically refused to permit any crossing at grade and there the matter rested until 1896.

# THE CYPRESS HILLS AND LUTHERAN LINES IN RIDGEWOOD
# THE BUSHWICK RAILROAD COMPANY

The oldest street railway routes in Brooklyn were conversions of old stage coach operations into rail lines. The old Kendall & Husted, Witty Bros., and Conselyea's stage coach lines became the nucleus of the Brooklyn City R. R.; Eckbert & Smith became the Broadway R. R. Similarly, the origin of the Bushwick R. R. is to be found in the stage coach line of M. B. Whittlesey & Co. which had its office in the 50's at number 4 So. 7th St.; his Omnibus House or stage depot stood on the south side of Broadway a little east of Sumner Ave. The old stables of the company were on the east side of Bushwick Ave. between Flushing Ave. and Monteith St., just about three blocks northeast of the Omnibus House. Passengers at the Omnibus House could board buses for Jamaica via Broadway and Jamaica Ave.; for East New York via the Hunterfly Road; and for Brooklyn via Broadway and Bedford Ave.

By the Civil War the old stage lines were gradually becoming obsolete. It was bad enough to bump along on the poorly surfaced roads of that day, but the small capacity of the vehicles doomed them in an age of expanding population. John Whittlesey, president of the stage lines, decided therefore to do what the more prosperous of the stage operators were doing in New York and Brooklyn, modernize by replacing his obsolescent stages with a horse railway.

In March 1860 the Brooklyn Common Council granted Whittlesey a franchise to construct a horse railroad running from the corner of Myrtle and Bushwick Avenues along Bushwick Ave., west along Meserole to So. 4th St., and then along So. 4th St. to Kent Ave. to So. 7th St., the terminus (Broadway Ferry). Returning, the cars were to go along So. 7th St. to Bedford Ave. and up Bedford to So. 4th St. Just as Whittlesey was about to build his road, the Civil War swept over the land and iron and timber became scarce or were bought up by the Federal Government for the war.

In December 1866 Whittlesey revived his project and requested and received permission from the Brooklyn Common Council to build his road; the old route of 1860 was reapproved and he was given until July 1, 1868 to open the line. On March 20, 1867 Whittlesey incorporated his new road as the Bushwick R. R. Company, and transferred to it his personal franchises.

On Sept. 20, 1867 the residents of So. 4th St. were greatly surprised to find material for a railroad piled up at intervals along the street, and a gang of laborers who were proceeding to tear up the pavement preparatory to laying track. Many of the residents who had given written consents in 1860 to build the line had moved away or died, and over the years new first class residences had been erected. Great indignation was expressed at the prospect of a street railway, and the next day measures were taken to secure an injunction against the company.

The following Monday, the 24th, the residents appeared in court to restrain the company on the ground that signatures had not been obtained as required by law; the company countered by pointing out that by the terms of a special legislative grant of 1866, it had been excepted from the usual provisions of the law. The judge seems to have been unimpressed and gave the company one week to show cause why the injunction should not be issued.

The hearing was postponed; meanwhile the property owners amassed a war chest. On Oct. 7th, 1867 the court denied the petition for an injunction on the strength of the railroad's special grants from the Legislature, which, the court ruled, had the power to turn over a street for railroad purposes. As soon as the snow and ice disappeared from the streets in the spring of 1868, construction began. By May 20 a double track railway had been completed from Broadway Ferry through So. 7th St., Bedford Ave., So. 4th St., Meserole St. and Bushwick Ave. to Myrtle Ave., and along Myrtle to Myrtle Ave. Park at Himrod St. On May 19th the first car, carrying the officials of the road, made a trial run from the old stage coach depot at Bushwick and Flushing Avenues to the foot of Broadway and return with complete success.

On Monday, June 1, 1868 the line was opened to the public. A connecting curve had been laid into Kent Ave. and cars ran on the Brooklyn City tracks as far as the Grand St. Ferry. The new road was four miles long and laid with 43 lb. rail. The 13 cars were all made by John Stephenson & Co. in New York, were painted yellow, and numbered 1-13. The cars were commended by the "Brooklyn Eagle" as quite an advance over those of other lines; they had platforms at either end and most modern feature of all, springs "so that in going over switches or turning curves, or on spots where the track is uneven or ill-jointed, there wil be none of the bumping and thumping which sometimes now takes the breathe out of passengers and creates a deafening noise." The cars were also the first to have wheel guards to clear obstacles from the track. The fare was 6 cents or 20 tickets for $1.

The new line was popularly called the "South 4th St. & Bowronville" line. The latter name has no meaning for us today but was familiar 100 years ago. In 1842 Watson Bowron (1807-1876) came to the Town of Bushwick and settled on a farm along what is now the north side of Evergreen Ave. between Menahan and Madison Streets. Here he opened a small dairy business. In 1852 he bought 40 acres of empty land north of his farm extending up to and along Myrtle Ave. and laid it out in building lots. He called the new development "Bowronville". The name subsequently came to be applied to all the land east of Flushing Ave. and north of Broadway. In 1869 the development had a paper of its own, and in an article of 1870 came in for considerable censure as a resort of gamblers in its half dozen hotels and saloons. By the 80's the city of Brooklyn began to absorb Bowronville and during the 90's it lost its identity completely to the growing suburb of Ridgewood.

In the spring of 1868 and again in 1870 the Bushwick R. R. planned an extension to Prospect Park, then being enlarged and just coming into its own as a pleasure retreat. This was to run via Broadway, Roebling St., Division Ave., Harrison St. and Tompkins Ave. to Fulton St., then south on Kingston and Prospect Place to the park. Political difficulties and competition from rival roads interfered with the plans and the line never quite reached Prospect Park.

Beginning in 1869 and for many years thereafter the company was capably managed by its president, Archibald M. Bliss. The Bliss family had been associated with Bushwick and Greenpoint for a century and more. Neziah Bliss in 1832 had all of what is now Greenpoint surveyed and laid out in city lots. The village of Blissville in Long Island City sprang up on what had been part of the family farm. Neziah's son, Archibald Bliss, not only managed the Bushwick R. R. but was prominent in politics; in 1870-71 he was Water Commissioner of Brooklyn, and assemblyman thereafter, and his father before him had served on the Board of Aldermen. This familiarity with politics and politicians must have been an invaluable asset for the young company.

From 1868 to 1874 the railroad mileage remained unchanged. These years were a period of growth and prosperity. Seven cars were bought in 1869, another in 1870, another in 1871, and eight in 1873. Passenger traffic had shown a splendid increase:

| 1868 (four mos.). | 342,955 | 1871 | 1,615,488 |
| 1869 | 1,122,396 | 1872 | 1,707,677 |
| 1870 | 1,236,719 | | |

On Dec 4, 1872 the company suffered a severe set-back through the loss of the Flushing Ave. stables due to a fire.

The company immediately set to work to rebuild the site with permanent and more substantial buildings; temporary sheds were put up to shelter the horses. On December 5th and 6th the company's only surviving car shuttled back and forth between the ferry and the stables. The Brooklyn City R. R. and the Brooklyn City & Newtown R. R. loaned several of their cars to tide the company over until new ones could be obtained. By the end of the year the company had again secured from John Stephenson 29 new cars at a cost of $25,000.

The new cars Bliss placed on the road were one-horse box cars, equipped with patent lock-box money receivers which eliminated the need for conductors, and so saved on wages and the losses incidental to "knocking down". The drivers, not having to bother with money, told reporters that they actually preferred these "jiggers" to two-man cars. In time, they even mastered a technique for "knocking down" on the new fare boxes. A friend accompanied the driver on his trips and sat himself next to the fare box, where he obligingly took the fares from the passengers, who thanked him for his courtesy. The friend then dropped a penny or button in the box, while the driver hastily pulled the cord to drop it out of sight of the glass window. The friend then pocketed the fare, and "whacked up" with the driver at the end of the day.

So prosperous did the Bushwick R. R. become, setbacks notwithstanding, that in 1875 the company was able to spend $97,500 for a new extension to Greenpoint. The new line branched off Meserole St. and continued up Graham Ave. to Driggs; along Driggs to Manhattan; and along Manhattan Ave. to Greenpoint Ave., and down Grenpoint Ave. to the ferry. To service this new 3 1/2 mile route, a new stable, repair shop and paint shop and smithy were erected on the site of the old stables at Bushwick Ave. and Monteith St., and sixteen new cars were secured from Stephenson, 12 Closed and four opens.

Excessively rainy weather in August 1875 slowed down the work of track laying, but the new route was finally opened and formally inspected by the directors of the company on Saturday, Sept. 18, 1875. A large open car, drawn by six of the company's finest horses, made the maiden trip from the Greenpoint Ferry to Myrtle Ave. Park. Pres. Bliss had been born and raised in Greenpoint, and his father, Neziah Bliss, had started the Greenpoint Ferry to 10th and 23rd Sts., New York, in 1852; his interest in that locality was therefore entirely understandable. The new extension was the first car line to tap the ferry traffic directly and to make possible crosstown travel between Greenpoint, Bushwick and Ridgewood.

Twenty cars were assigned to the new route, running on about a seven minute headway. All Greenpoint cars ran out of Bushwick car barn, and to distinguish them from the So. 4th St. and Meserole cars, they were painted green and carried a green light at night. This was doubly appropriate: the car served not only the Greenpoint district, but an almost purely Irish neighborhood.

Bliss, at the time that he had laid out the Greenpoint line, had never intended that it should serve Greenpoint alone. He had conceived of the extension as but the northern end of a long crosstown route that should extend southward through Graham and Tompkins Ave. to Prospect Park. The vast Bedford-Stuyvesant area south of Bushwick and east of Brooklyn was in the 70's being rapidly settled, and the local traffic, plus the through park traffic seemed to insure the success of an extension through that area. Tentative plans by the Bushwick R. R. to build roads southward involved Tompkins Ave. as early as 1868, Reid and Utica Avenues in 1870, and Sumner and Troy Avenues in 1875, and Kingston Ave. and St. Marks Place in 1878-79. All of these plans proved abortive except the first, and even when finally built, the Tompkins Ave. line proved not the lower end of a through crosstown route, but an independent line out of Broadway Ferry.

Work was begun on the construction of the Tompkins Ave. route on April 14, 1876. The project had hardly progressed any distance when the property owners along Division Ave. protested against the laying of tracks because the street had just been repaved; reassurances that the damages would be made good did not altogether convince the residents. By the middle of June tracks had been almost completely laid through Broadway, Roebling, Division, Harrison and Tompkins Ave. On the southeast corner of Fulton St. and Brooklyn Ave. the company erected a large stable to accommodate horses and cars of the new line. It had originally been expected to open the new road in mid-June, but a quarrel broke out with the Williamsburgh & Flatbush R. R. Co., operators of the Nostrand Ave. line, over the location of turnouts to Broadway Ferry. The Brooklyn Common Council, in order to clear the center of Broadway of the waiting horse cars of all the companies, had arranged two long turnouts, one on each side of the street, where the cars of all companies terminating at Broadway Ferry might stand. The Nostrand Ave. company objected to moving from its old stand on the north side of Broadway. The city secured an injunction to force removal, but the company carried through its own switching changes on Saturday night and over Sunday to forestall legal interference. By July 4th the Nostrand Ave. company had vacated the terminal area assigned to the Bushwick R. R., and the company was able to lay a turnout in front of No. 15 Broadway.

In the first week of July 1876 it was announced that the new line would open soon; 16 new two-horse cars, both open and closed, arrived meanwhile from the Stephenson factory to stock the new route. On July 10th the first car went over the new Tompkins

Ave. route. Immediate success was predicted for the new line inasmuch as it passed the Union and Capitoline Baseball Grounds, and the Lefferts and Tompkins Parks. The length of the road was about 2-3/4 miles and was all double tracked; 14 cars were assigned for duty between 5 a.m. and 12 p.m. on a headway of from five to eight minutes. Two days later on Thursday, July 13, 1876, the new Tompkins line was thrown open to the public.

The Bushwick R.R.'s latest route branched off at 7th St. and Bedford Ave., ran on Broadway to Roebling St., south on Roebling to Division St., then south on Harrison St. and Tompkins Ave. to Fulton St. All Tompkins cars operated out of the Tompkins Depot; were painted maroon and carried a maroon light for night identification.

In 1877 the Bushwick R.R. crossed into Queens County for the first time. For nine years the company had been operating along Myrtle Ave. from Bushwick Ave. to the part at Himrod St. At this early date Myrtle Ave. above Broadway was a dirt road with truck farms and empty lots on either side. In the neighborhood of the city line there were but two things to attract patronage: Welz & Zerweck's Brewery near Wyckoff Ave., which was established in 1861, and Union Cemetery between Knickerbocker, Irving, Palmetto and Putnam Avenues, opened in 1851, and closed in 1897. Eight blocks short of the city line on the north side of Myrtle Ave. was Myrtle Avenue Park, the terminus of the Brooklyn City R.R.'s Myrtle Ave. line from the downtown ferries.

In June 1854, a new Myrtle Ave. opened; it began at the old limit of settlement at Broadway. Here stood the Franklin Hotel since colonial days. For decades passengers bound for Bowronville and East New York had enjoyed the hospitality of the old hotel where they changed coaches.

The Brooklyn City R.R. reached the hotel a few months after the opening of a new turnpike to Jamaica. In July 1854 sixteen cars opened the new Myrtle Ave. line between Fulton Ferry and the old stage coach stables, newly remodeled for horse cars, at Myrtle and Marcy Avenues. By November the line had been completed to Broadway, and three "transfer" cars carried passengers from Marcy Ave. stables to the Franklin Hotel.

The opening of the Myrtle Ave. plank road and the horse car line produced great changes. The old hotel, once surrounded by farms, gradually found itself hemmed in by stores and houses. In 1859 the Broadway R.R. began operating horse cars along Broadway; in July 1869 the line opened a large new depot at Myrtle and Broadway. By the time the Bushwick R.R. appeared on the scene in 1877, Myrtle Ave. had already experienced 20 years of intensive development. Only the area east of Myrtle Ave. Park lay open for further development.

When the Bushwick R.R. moved into this open area in 1877, it was actuated by motives other than meeting the competition of other roads. Barely two miles away beyond the city line lay two great sources of potenial revenue, the Lutheran Cemetery and the Cypress Hills Cemetery. The company that tapped these sites first would be guaranteed cemetery patronage for decades to come. The Bushwick R. R. resolved to seize the initiative.

Before construction could begin an important obstacle had first to be overcome. Myrtle Ave. was a turnpike road owned by private interests and the charter was not due to expire until 1883. Either the turnpike owners would have to be induced to permit the laying of a track, or else they would have to be bought out. Fortunately for the railroad company, the county was at this very moment considering buying out the turnpike bondholders and converting Myrtle Ave. into a public road. In February 1875 Senator Oakley offered to the Legislature a bill providing for the purchase, widening and improvement of the Myrtle Ave. Plank Road; three Commissioners were to assess damages and no more than $4000 was to be paid to the owners. Any rails on the highways were to be laid on either side, at least 15ft. apart; the Brooklyn City and Bushwick R. R. both showed keen interest in the plan. At first the supervisors were opposed to the improvement because it would create debt for the Town, but a series of lawsuits compelled action. It was charged that one of the supervisors had been paid to oppose the improvement by a group financially interested in the Jamaica Ave. Plank Road. If Myrtle Ave. were made into a free route to Brooklyn, many Long Island farmers would stop using Jamaica Ave. as an outlet to the Brooklyn markets. The Jamaica Ave. people were getting a 14 cent toll for a team and wagon, and it was estimated that the average farmer was then paying 50 to 75 dollars per year for the use of this through highway.

By the spring of 1877 all the obstacles, both political and legal, had been cleared away and work began on Aug. 21, 1877 at the Brooklyn end. The Bushwick R. R. followed hot on the heels of the pavers. T-rails were laid from the old terminus at Myrtle Ave. Park as far as Stroebel's Hotel at Cypress Ave. during mid-November 1877. On Thursday, November 29th, service opened as far as High Ground Park at Grove St.

The spring of 1878 saw great innovations on the Bushwick R. R. service. The opening of the new line at Stroebel's Hotel was but the first step. The next was to continue the railroad along Cypress Ave. to the cemetery gates. Like Myrtle Ave., Cypress Ave. had begun its existence as a private toll road in the 50's under the name "Williamsburgh and Cypress Hills Plank Road."

The Bushwick R. R. must have come to terms with the owners of the Cypress Ave. plank road, for, on April 4, 1878, ground was broken for the extension of the railroad from Stroebel's Hotel on Myrtle Ave. to the cemetery gates. In the short space of one week the rails were laid along the whole road. It was at this point that the Bushwick R. R. surprised everyone by announcing that the new Cypress Hills Branch would be operated by steam dummies. Had the line opened a few years earlier or a few years later, horse cars would undoubtedly have served the traffic, but in the Brooklyn of 1877 and 1878, the reputation of the steam dummy was at its height, and the adoption of this mode of propulsion was considered the latest and most progressive move possible.

The South Side R. R. of Long Island seemed to have started the idea in Brooklyn; its depot was on the edge of the settled area at Bushwick Ave. and at this point, the passenger coaches were uncoupled from the steam engines, and coupled to small enclosed dummy engines, which hauled the big railroad coaches through Boerum St. and Broadway to the So. 8th St. terminus. The use of horses for drawing street cars was admittedly unsatisfactory, and most street railway executives were on the alert for a cheap, efficient substitute. Most officials hesitated to experiment in the congested city streets where accidents were frequent and expensive, but for suburban routes the idea seemed safe and attractive. The Brooklyn City R. R. was the first to try out dummy operation on its Third Avenue line between 25th St. and Ft. Hamilton in August of 1877. The idea proving a success, the Brooklyn City and Broadway R. R. jointly opened a steam dummy line along Fulton St. in East New York in June 1878.

The apparent success of these two attempts was sufficient to make a favorable impression on the Bushwick R.R. officials and they determined to adopt the new method for the cemetery branch. The dummy needed only one operator, did not send up objectionable clouds of smoke, was immune to diseases and heat, and best of all, could draw several cars at once during periods of peak load on Sundays and holidays. The first step was to select a site for an engine house; the site selected was on Myrtle Ave. diagonally opposite Myrtle Ave. Park, between Harmon St. and Greene Ave.

The first order for steam dummies was placed in November or December 1877, and by the first week in February 1878, three dummies were in the company's possession.

In March 1878 the Bushwick R.R. placed an additional order for two dummies with the Baldwin Locomotive Works,; they were delivered on May 17th. All five bore the names of the local cemeteries enroute. With five dummies on hand the company was ready to begin the new service. On Sunday, May 26, the new

BRT open bench car No 1810.

Cypress Hills line was opened. The horse cars that had been running to Stroebel's Hotel were removed, and all city horse cars terminated their runs at Myrtle Ave. Park at Harmon St. and Myrtle Ave. Patrons for the cemetery crossed the street to the new depot and boarded the dummy or one of the trailer cars, paying the extra 3 cent fare. The dummy took 12 minutes to make the two mile trip to the cemetery gate.

The great success of the Cypress Hills Branch convinced the company that a second branch to the cemetery would be equally profitable. Between the city line and the Lutheran Cemetery stretched an unbroken succession of farmlands; no villages intervened and no streets interrupted the open countryside. In the spring of 1880 rumors spread that the Bushwick R.R. planned to extend the dummy line along Myrtle Ave. to Glendale. The company was negotiating for a right of way between Myrtle Ave. and the Lutheran Cemetery, and for a depot site opposite the cemetery entrance. By December 1880 a site had been secured on the south side of Metropolitan Ave., the site is still familiar today as the Myrtle Ave. elevated terminal.

By the end of February 1881 the company had pieced together a right of way direct from the new Ridgewood depot to the Lutheran Cemetery. The spring months witnessed intensive activity on both the new right of way and the depot. The Depot building was planned on a large scale so that it would serve for years to come as the general depot for all lines.

Progress on the new depot was brisk. By June the building was well along, and so much special work was being installed in the street that the papers complained that the macadamized road

31

was disappearing in a wilderness of switches and sidings. A third track was laid in front of the depot and only a month later did it occur to the officials to ask permission to install it!

By the first of August the new line was so far completed that operation was expected in two weeks. The depot at the cemetery was being fitted up and painted. By late August the new depot at Ridgewood was so far advanced that the steam dummies occupied the new facilities and the small barn opposite Myrtle Avenue Park was given up. On Aug. 28th the horse cars began to run from the ferries all the way to the new depot, and steam service operated only between the depot and the Cypress Hill Cemetery, i.e., within Queens County only. Meanwhile the new rolling stock for the Lutheran line began arriving and was housed in the new depot.

On Saturday, Sept. 3, 1881, the Lutheran line opened. A crowd of about 100 people assembled at the new Ridgewood depot in response to the invitation of the Bushwick R.R. management to be present at the formal ceremonies opening the new line. At 4 p.m. a two car train, gaily trimmed with flags and bunting, started out from the depot. The spectators crowded into the cars and watched as the little train passed through the high

Brooklyn City dummy No 8 brought up from Ft. Hamilton for use on the Lutheran and Cyrpess Hills line, from 1889 to 1895. These were larger than the Bushwick R.R. dummies, there is a 13 window coach in the backround. *Vincent F. Seyfried collection.*

banks just north of the depot, and then along the long embankment east and west of Fresh Pond Rd., the high iron bridge over the LIRR and finally pulled into the new wooden terminal opposite the main gate of the Lutheran Cemetery. After a short tour of the "new and commodious" depot, the company returned to the Ridgewood depot, into which all were invited to partake of a banquet served by caterers. Toward the end of the meal Mr. S. L. Husted, a relative of the president spoke. Thirty-six years before he had started the first stage coach line in Brooklyn between Fulton Ferry and Broadway. He traced the growth of Brooklyn from a city of 40,000 to 700,000 and reviewed the growth of transit. Other short speeches followed, and at the end, all the employees of the road were treated to a supper.

The new Lutheran Line was well constructed and a credit to the company. It was double tracked throughout, except across the LIRR bridge; the coaches were all new from the workshops of Pratt & Co. of Philadelphia and Stephenson in New York. They were painted a dark red. The dummies now eight in number, were all from the Baldwin Locomotive Works. All were named as well as numbered, the custom of the steam roads of the day. Turntables were built into the street at each end of the line to turn the dummies. A ride over the 1 1/2 mile line took eight minutes and the fare was 5 cents, or 3 cents for children.

Though the Lutheran line opened rather late in the season, it was a big success from the start. The newness of the equipment, the speed of the service and the novelty of the dummy attracted many patrons. Many cemetery visitors, disgusted with the undependable service on the Metropolitan Ave. horse car, and the old, dirty cars, flocked to the dummy as a faster and more comfortable mode of travel. There was but one complaint against the new line: the fare was too high. Passengers had to pay 5 cents on horse cars to the city line and then 5 cents more on the dummy. Even the Cypress Hills route, which was one-quarter mile longer, charged only 3 cents. The 10 cents fare notwithstanding, patronage was heavy and three-car trains were required to accommodate the traffic.

At the same time that the Bushwick R.R. was developing the cemetery traffic the Brooklyn City R.R. resolved to tap the Ridgewood area. In April 1881 the company purchased 38 city lots on the southeast corner of Wyckoff Ave. and Palmetto St. for a large new depot, diagonally across the street from the Bushwick R.R. depot. By September the big new terminus was finished and it immediately became the depot for two lines of horse cars, the routes of which were extended to it: Gates Ave., and Myrtle Ave. On Aug. 27, 1881 the Brooklyn City road extended its Myrtle Ave. line from the old terminus at Myrtle Avenue Park to Ridgewood Park. The Bushwick R.R.'s dummies turned off Myrtle Ave. into Cypress Ave., but the Brooklyn City horse cars ran along Myrtle Ave. a few feet further east, then turned into the park grounds itself, where sidings were built to accommodate excursion crowds.

Ridgewood Park normally remained closed during the winter months and cars stopped at the depot. When the park opened, usually about May 15th, cars ran through to the park. On Special picnic days the Brooklyn City charged 5 cents for a through ride between the ferries and the park, but at all other times there was an extra 3 cent charge for a ride beyond the county line. Many were the complaints of the Ridgewood residents about the 8 cent fare.

The presence of both depots at the city line made Ridgewood a major railroad terminus almost overnight; six lines converged at the twin depots. The recent macadamizing of Myrtle Ave. along with the new railroads sparked several changes in the neighborhood. In January 1881, Fred Stroebel having died a few months before, the valuable hotel was auctioned off and sold to his son-in-law, John Kreuscher, who continued to operate it. Thanks to its enviable situation, it was considered one of the most valuable in Queens County.

As the 80's wore on, the prosperity of the Bushwick R.R. continued. Whenever the holidays and summer weekends coincided with good weather, people boarded the cars in droves. Decoration Day, Pfingst Monday, July 4th and Labor Day drew crowds to the parks and beer gardens to enjoy the rural scenery and pleasures and witness the performances of turners and singing societies. Traffic must have been appreciable even in winter for the dummies drew trailers all winter long. When the snows got too deep, passengers were carried in the dummy itself.

As the 80's drew to a close additional improvements were made on all the properties, both city and suburban. The Tompkins Ave. line in the Bedford area was extended 1 1/2 miles in 1878. Instead of terminating at the new depot on Fulton St., cars ran half a block east to Kingston Ave., down Kingston Ave. to Bergen St. and west along Bergen to the Bergen St. depot, then located between Classon and Franklin Avenues. Since September 1866 horse cars had been running along Bergen St. and the depot had been opened at that time to accommodate the cars. This extension not only provided connections with the Nostrand, Franklin and Bergen lines of cars, but came to within three blocks of the boundaries at that time of Prospect Park. In 1883 service was cut back for some reason to Kingston and Atlantic Avenues, but in 1885 was extended to Kingston and Bergen again. No further changes in the Tompkins Ave. line were made thereafter.

The Greenpoint line also received some attention. In 1882 the line was lengthened from 3.75 miles to 4.34 miles from which we can infer that service was extended out to the new Myrtle Ave. stables. It seems reasonable to suppose that the old Bushwick Ave. depot at Flushing Ave. was abandoned at this time.

In 1882 both the Bushwick and Greenpoint lines received new rolling stock under pressure of public opinion.

The change for the better must have been long overdue. The older cars were "bob-tail" equipment, short boxes with only one platform, and drawn by only one horse, the driver being the entire crew. Brooklyn, especially Williamsburgh and Bushwick, had long since outgrown this obsolete and limited service, and required 16 and 18 ft. cars with two platforms and seven or eight windows if the minimum needs of the traveling public were to be met.

In May 1883 the papers were able to joyfully announce that "the bobtail cars on the Greenpoint & Bushwick lines are things of the past, two-horse cars having taken their place." The improvement in rolling stock was followed by a renewal of the rail of all that part of the Greenpoint line owned by the Bushwick R.R., i.e., the stretch along Greenpoint Ave. from the ferry up to Manhattan Ave., 1,625 ft. in all. The final improvement on the Greenpoint line was the installation in 1887 of two open cars for the increased summer travel.

The Bushwick R.R. embarked upon its final expansion in 1885 with the opening of a 1.16 mile extension along Knickerbocker Ave., Ridgewood, from Myrtle Ave. to Flushing Ave. and along Flushing to Bushwick Ave., permission for which had been granted by the Common Council on Feb. 26, 1885. This branch appears to have been operated as a shuttle, though Bushwick Ave. cars could have used it as an alternate route to the depot at the city line.

The steam dummy lines came in for their share of improvements as well. In 1885 the Lutheran Line was enclosed by wire fences and in 1886 additional land was bought for track facilities. The Cypress Hills dummy line was improved in 1885 with 2,400 ft. of new track, and the location of the sidings was changed at the same time, eight years' experience having demonstrated the need of relocation. The following year - 1886 - saw the installation of additional sidings for the summer crowds at Ridgewood Park.

The Bushwick R.R. company leased its entire road and equipment to the Brooklyn City RR. The lease took effect Aug. 1, 1888; by its terms the Brooklyn City R.R. undertook to operate the Bushwick lines for 999 years and guaranteed to pay the annual dividend of 7% and to pay all interest on debts.

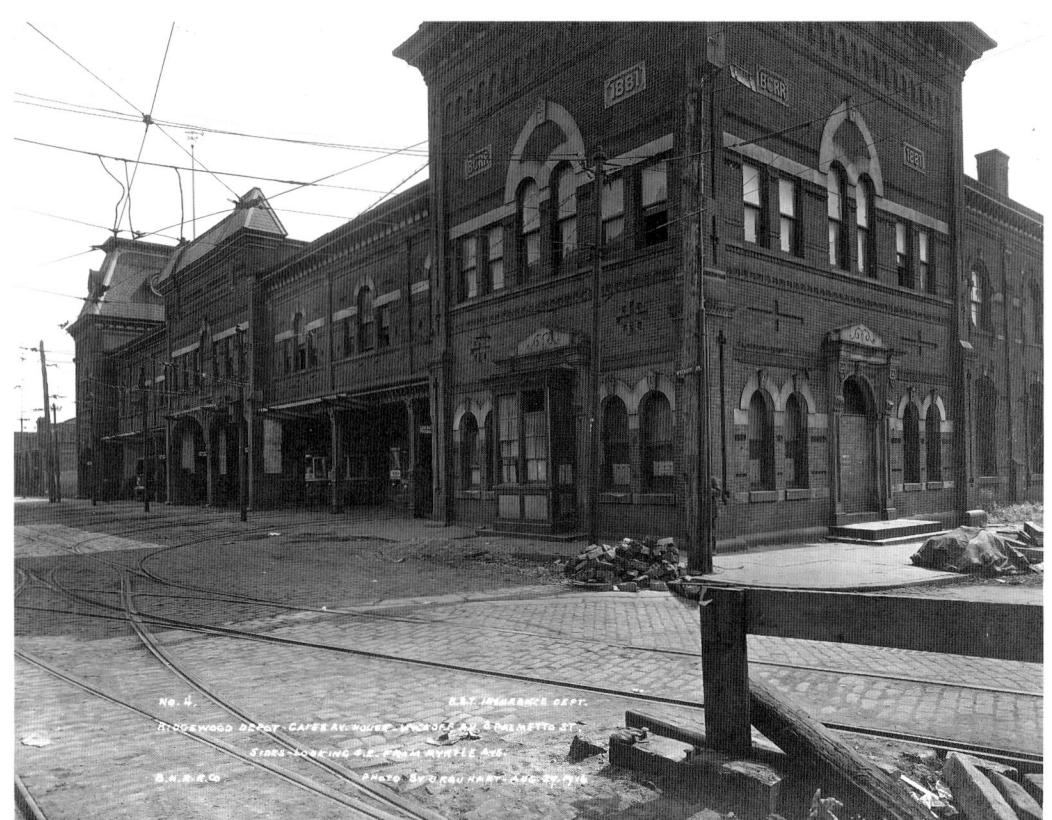

*Upper Left:* Ridgewood Depot, Gates Ave. house, Wyckoff Ave. and Palmetto St. Looking south-east from Myrtle Ave., August 29, 1916.
*Above:* Ridgewood Depot, 1906.
*Below:* Ridgewood Depot, March 6, 1925
All photos, *Robert Presbrey collection.*

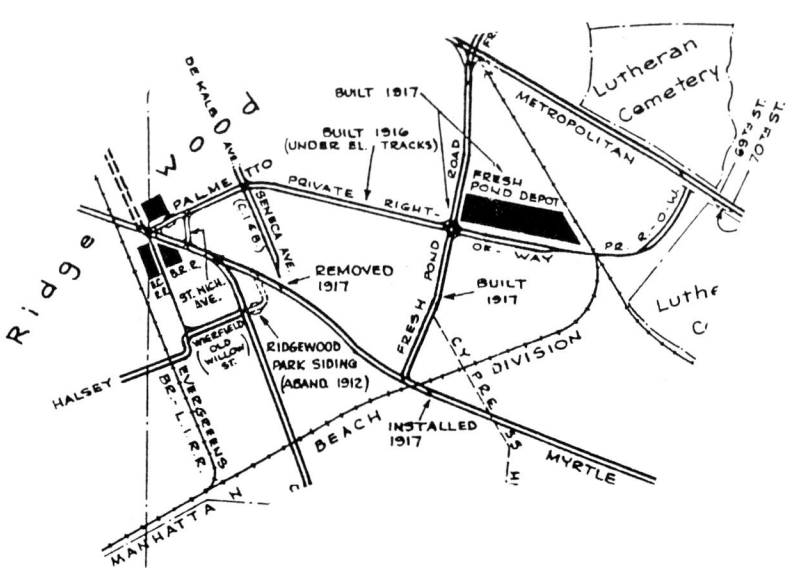

Old Bushwick R.R. Depot, at the corner of Palmetto St. and Myrtle Ave. 1881. Edward Watson collection.

1914 photo of Maspeth Depot, at Grand Ave. & Brown Pl. *Robert Presbrey* photo.

# ELECTRIFICATION OF GRAND ST. & EXTENSION TO NORTH BEACH

The year 1893 is memorable in local street railway history not only for the addition of many new miles of routes in Queens, but for the first extensive electrification of the Brooklyn City system. Because of the novelty of the system and the doubt on the part of many prominent street railway executives that electricity could propel cars as efficiently and as cheaply as horse power, the first electric line had been started on Jamaica Ave. on a trial basis on Dec. 17, 1887 by a private operator. The success of the new system was immediate and decisive, and it was thereafter just a matter of time and money before all the lines were equipped with electric power.

The decision to adopt the trolley was a radical and costly step for the Brooklyn Heights system. In effect, it meant the scrapping of their entire investment and a total reconstruction of the properties. At one stroke the cars became obsolete and had to be replaced by larger and heavier built bodies able to carry electrical equipment. Miles of copper wire had to be strung through the streets, supported by miles of iron span wires, and to suspend them, thousands of iron poles had to be installed. The old horse car rails, uneven in weight and often poorly joined, had to be bonded before the electric cars could begin running. Finally, large power houses and sub-stations had to be built to supply the electrical needs of an extensive and ever-expanding system.

In spite of these heavy demands on the Brooklyn Heights treasury, electrification proceeded with astonishing rapidity. Hamilton Ave. was electrified on June 1, 1892; Court St. on December 26, 1892; and Third Ave. on November 7, 1892. In the spring of 1893 the lines out of downtown Brooklyn were opened, Flatbush Ave. on March 13, Fulton St. on June 7, Gates Ave. on June 23, Putnam Ave. on July 17, and Myrtle Ave. on August 22.

In the fall of 1893 the trolley made its first appearance in Williamsburgh and Greenpoint. On September 2nd Greenpoint was electrified, Flushing Ave. on October 1st, and Bushwick Ave. on December 11th. Completion of the electrification through all North Brooklyn was dependent upon the opening of the new power house being constructed on Kent Ave., the largest of its kind in the world at the time with a capacity of 10,000 HP.

In August 1893 the work of electrification of Grand Ave. began with the stringing of wires along the Williamsburgh end. At the same time the Maspeth Depot was being readied for the reception of electric cars; extensive interior alterations were made, and the roof of the car bays was raised several feet to allow for cars with trolley poles to run into the building. A large new waiting

North Beach bathing area c.1896. Note that all bathers are men! *P. Geifel photo.*

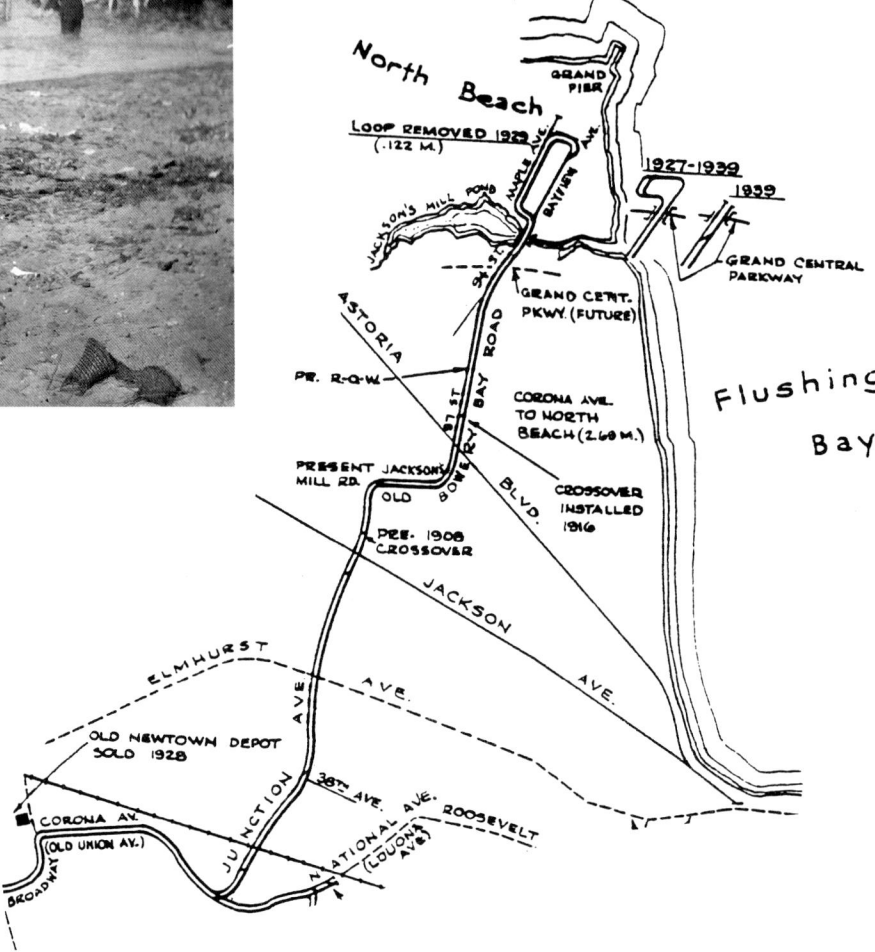

room with all conveniences was also added. By October nearly the whole of the Grand St. line to Newtown Creek, and the branch on Meeker Ave. had been strung with trolley wire. In the first week of October the Grand St. horse car drivers were summoned to Brooklyn and given practice in driving trolleys on the electrified routes.

On Sunday morning, March 25, 1894 a Flushing Ave. car was switched from the Graham Ave. tracks to Grand St., and run all the way out to Corona and back. Foreman George Robinson of the Newtown line acted as motorman; the car, loaded with company officers, passed over the Newtown Creek bridge without incident. All along the line the car was greeted with cheers; it was the first Brooklyn City trolley to enter Queens County and everyone saw it as the symbol of a new age of progress. On May 20 the citizens of Maspeth were startled to see a procession of 16 handsome trolleys rolling along Grand St. towards the Maspeth Depot. On Monday, May 21st, these new cars opened regular service on Grand St. from the Maspeth Depot to the Broadway ferries.

On Sunday, May 27th, one week after the Grand St. line opened, trolley cars began running between Maspeth depot and Junction Ave. Corona, and four days later, on May 31, 1894, the first trip was made over the road to Bowery Bay. Again George Robinson piloted the car, and among the passengers was President Lewis himself of the Brooklyn Heights R.R. and the superintendent of Newtown. When the car reached Jackson's Mill, a stop was made, and the party toured the old mill, its great water wheel and grind stones still in tact. Then the car proceeded to Flushing Bay where the party stopped for dinner. That afternoon they returned to Brooklyn, very pleased with the new route.

The following day, Friday, June 1, 1894, regular service began on the Bowery Bay line. As then operated, cars ran through from the Broadway ferries through Kent Ave., Grand Ave., Corona Ave. and Junction Ave. to the beach. The distance was 9 miles and the trip took 45 minutes. It had been the intention of the Brooklyn City operating division to make the Bowery Bay line run out of Ridgewood depot along the Lutheran right of way, Fresh Pond Rd., Grand St., Corona Ave. and Junction Ave. to the beach, but because of the failure to resolve the Fresh Pond crossing, the line was forced to operate the new line as part of the Grand St. route.

On the first Sunday, June 3rd, between seven and eight thousand passengers, mostly from the city, were carried to North Beach and back. On the following Sunday, June 10th, four thousand fares were run up on the Grand St. cars going to Bowery Bay. For a single 5 cent fare residents of North Brooklyn had access for the first time to a beach front and amusement park, and they turned out in droves to take advantage of it.

Bowery Bay at this date was the newest pleasure resort in the city. It had been incorporated in April 1886 by piano manufacturer, William Steinway, and the brewer George Ehret, with the intention of making it a rival of Coney Island. In May 1886 development began, and in a very short time, what had been an unspoiled beach front blossomed with recreational buildings of all kinds. By the end of 1886 there was a pavilion and over 100 bath houses. In 1887 Grand Pier was built off Sanford's Point, 400 ft. long and 150 ft. wide, designed to accommodate steamers from New York, the Bronx and College Point. By 1890 four summer ferries plied regularly between Grand Pier and Morrisania, 130th St. and 3rd Ave., and College Point. The street railways from Long Island City reached the beach in June 1890, and Sanford's Point in May 1887. By the time the Brooklyn City R.R. reached the resort, it had already become very well known to residents of North Queens and was drawing as many as 10,000 visitors every Sunday. Its attractions included a club house, pavilion, music, a merry-go-round, a steam roller coaster, dancing, quaint old world villages, beer halls and Silver Lake, an artificial creation for salt water swimming. In February 1891 the owners changed the name to North Beach, and it was under this name that it became famous over the next 30 years.

As the Brooklyn City's new Bowery Bay line became more familiar to patrons, traffic stabilized at about 25,000 passengers per Sunday. The ride along this route was wonderfully rural and refreshing to the inhabitants of crowded Williamsburgh. By 1894 the old Brooklyn section had been solidly built up eastward through Bushwick and out into Ridgewood and Maspeth.

Once a rider left Maspeth, the open country began. Scattered homes only bordered the road until one reached Newtown Village, now Elmhurst; east of Newtown lay Corona, a small village with a few homes and commercial buildings. Once the car turned north into Junction Ave. and the Bowery Bay Rd., all vestiges of settlement were left behind. Fields and farms stretched in all directions, most tilled by the descendants of the original Dutch settlers, Rapalje, Kouwenhoven, Sanford etc. Trees overhung the two tracks and only an occasional farm wagon or farm house interrupted the unspoiled landscape.

After Astoria Blvd. (old Flushing Ave) was crossed, the land gently descended until one went sharply downhill and crossed the little bridge over Jackson's Mill Pond. A little stream that drained the area formerly known as Train's Meadow (now Jackson Heights) was impounded here by a tidewater gate creating a pond, beside which stood old Jackson's Mill, a relic of colonial times.

Queens County trolley operations in this first year of electrification proved to be challenge to the ridership. The extreme end of the line in Corona east of Junction Ave was still being operated by horses. The company ran a single one horse car from Junction Ave. out to Corona station along Corona and National Avenues. This service ran without regard to any schedule or public convenience. Since the car ran uncertainly, one had to wait at Junction Ave., without the benefit of shelter of any kind from the elements. At nite there was no light of any kind except that of a house near by.

During Christmas week of 1894 the Brooklyn City R.R. published its first trolley schedule in the papers. The cars left Maspeth Depot for Corona every 20 minutes, every 45 minutes for Jackson Ave., and hourly for Bowery Bay between 11 a.m. and 9 p.m. only. In all there were 63 trips a day between Maspeth Depot and Corona, eight morning and three night trips to Jackson Ave. and 10 trips a day through Bowery Bay.

Both the Brooklyn City R.R. and the various lines it purchased, all had bought new batches of horse cars at regular intervals down to 1889. When electrification started on an extensive scale in 1891-92, many of these cars were still new and in serviceable condition, and it was decided that, rather than scrap a large capital investment prematurly, it would pay to convert the best cars to elecric operation. For this purpose, in 1891-93 they purchased truck frames and motors from Westinghouse, Dupont, Peckham and General Electric. The truck frames were bolted under the car bodies, and controllers installed on the front and rear platforms, the cars were then wired and roofs reinforced to support trolley poles.

A roster of cars might have looked like this:
Cars #1-1699 were largely confined to Brooklyn routes.
Cars #1700-4400 were assigned to Queens County.
All odd number series were closed cars.
All even number series were open cars.
There was often a certain amount of variation even within any one number series, so it is difficult to make any completely accurate generalizations about these early cars. All the cars were single truck, the closed cars having between 5 and 8 windows, and horse car "turtle-back" roofs. The open cars had from 7 to 11 benches, nearly always back-to-back and immovable. Destination signs were affixed on the front and rear bonnets and the sides at roof level. For night operation the cars carried kerosene lamps as head lights.

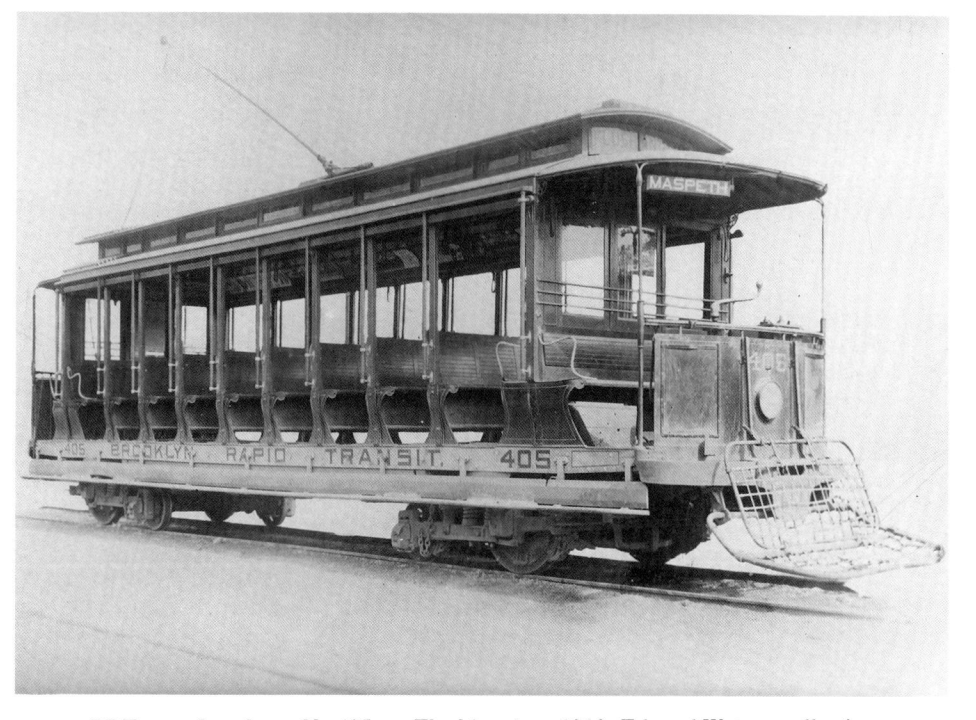

BRT open bench car No 405, on Flushing Ave. 1910. *Edward Watson collection.*

Many extensions were planned but never built, probably because resources were already strained reequipping and electrifying 200 miles of existing system. The proposed extensions were in two general areas, the first north and east of Corona, the second all across north central Queens. On December 19, 1892 franchises were granted for:
1. Along Elmhurst Ave. from Junction Ave. to Northern Blvd.
2. Along National Ave. from Corona Ave. to Roosevelt Ave. and along Roosvelt Ave to 114th St., and up 114th St. to Elmhurst Ave., and along Elmhurst Ave. to Northern Blvd.

On October 31, 1893 they were granted franchises for:
1. Along Queens Blvd. from Greenpoint Ave. to 83rd Ave.
2. Along Laurel Hill Blvd. from Penny Bridge, Long Island City to Queens Blvd. and along 45th Ave. and Elmhurst Ave. to Junction Ave.
3. Along 58th St. from Laurel Hill Blvd. to Roosevelt Ave. in Woodside.
4. Along Celtic Ave. from the junction of Laurel Hill Blvd. and 42nd St., to the intersection of Queens Blvd. and Roosevelt Ave.
5. All along Woodhaven Blvd. from Queens Blvd. to just north of Jamaica Ave.

Some of these franchise routes were highly visionary considering the date they were granted. The routes could not have originated sufficient revenue to sustain a trolley line, but optimism and unlimited belief in the future development of empty Queens farm land into home sites were the driving force. It was considered prudent to invest in franchises on the few existing through streets in the hope of future profits.

## THE DUMMY COMES TO RICHMOND HILL

We have seen how the Bushwick R.R. was instrumental in the growth of the new suburb of Ridgewood by inaugurating its steam dummy service beyond the county line into Queens. This growth was further accelerated by the electrification of the Ridgewood trolley lines and the other long lines that had their terminal there.

In 1893, the Brooklyn City R.R. made its first move to electrify the Ridgewood lines by constructing a large power plant on Wyckoff Ave. in April 1893. In the summer the first electric cars came to Ridgewood; Greene and Gates Ave. on June 23rd; Myrtle Ave. on August 21st; and Bushwick Ave. December 11th. As electrification was proceeding all through Brooklyn, the steam dummies operating on the two suburban lines remained unaffected.

In the summer of 1891 the Brooklyn City R.R. suprised everyone by proposing to extend the Myrtle Ave. line far out into the suburbs, all the way to Jamaica, where Myrtle Ave. joined Jamaica Ave. in the small village of Richmond Hill.

In mid-July they applied to the Town of Jamaica for permission to lay tracks from the Town Line at Lefferts Ave. eastward to Jamaica Ave. The franchise was granted with the following terms; double tracks were to be laid and the street paved for a width of 18 ft. with block pavement. The road would be operated by steam motors for 3 years, and then electric cars would be substituted. The road had to be in operation by January 1893, and the fare from Richmond Hill to the Brooklyn ferries was set at 5 cents.

The work of building the line began the first week of February 1892, and by the end of April 500 men were at work. One track had been completed through to Richmond Hill; the other track had reached Fresh Pond Rd.

The opening of the line took place on May 27, 1892. At 3:30 p.m. the dummy "George B. McCellan" dew out of the Ridgewood station with two gaily decorated cars. The run over the four miles to Richmond Hill was made in 17 minutes, including three stops.

The following day, regular service began over the Myrtle Ave. extension; the weekday headway was 12 minutes and on Sunday 10 minutes. On the first Sunday of operation 2,500 people rode the new line.

In the last week of June 1892 the Brooklyn Heights R.R. published the first time table for the dummy operation to Richmond Hill in the local Jamaica newspaper. One of the immediate effects of the new line along Myrtle Ave. was the opening of beer gardens and "Schuetzen Parks" or pistol ranges along the road.

As the Ridgewood power plant drew to completion in the fall of 1893, plans were made for the electrification of the three steam dummy lines out of Ridgewood Depot. In August 1893 the poles, span wire and trolley wires were being strung along lower Myrtle Ave. in Ridgewood and electric cars began running on August 21st.

With the coming of the new year 1894, the first installation of poles and wire on the Queens side of Ridgewood was undertaken along Cypress Ave. out to the cemetery. Thereafter, no further attempt was made to extend the trolley system. The effort to electrify 9 miles of Grand St. and all the way out to Bowery Bay taxed the full resources of the Brooklyn City R.R. and offered far greater certainty of immediate return than the three short suburban runs out of Ridgewood.

# HIGH FINANCES AND HOT FIGHTING

The year 1895 was probably the most eventful and stirring year in the history of the Brooklyn traction system. It was a year that witnessed within the span of a few months the rise and collapse of a gigantic financial maneuver planned to extract millions from a new and expanding traction empire, and, on the other hand, the most violent and bitterly contested strike in the history of street railweays.

The 80's and 90's were a period of merger and consolidation in industry everywhere in America, and this was especially true in the traction industry of Manhattan and Brooklyn. The initial impetus in this direction was taken in Brooklyn by a group of bankers who had studied the street railway industry on a national basis, and came to the conclusion that the traction field was good for investment and expansion. On March 21, 1887, the bankers syndicate incorporated the Brooklyn Heights R.R. and secured a franchise to operate a one-mile cable line on Montague St., Brooklyn, from the East River to Fulton St. The Montague St. line was intended from the first as the necessary short stretch of track to qualify the company as a railway company; once this was accomplished, the organization would then act as a holding company, buying or leasing as many surface systems as possible. In February 1892 the short Montague St. line was opened for business.

The next step in the complex process of unification was the leasing for 999 years of the Brooklyn City R.R. to the Brooklyn Heights on February 14, 1893, the lease to take effect from June 6th. In this way the new syndicate acquired at one stroke the largest street railway system in Brooklyn, the Brooklyn City having already having merged some of the smaller companies into itself in the previous years. The merger also had the effect of bringing together the bankers and experienced street railway operators into a united organization.

To further their aims without incurring excessive taxes on capitalization, and to evade the supervision of the State Securities Commission, the bankers and directors did an extraordinary thing. They traveled to Virginia, and incorporated there on March 10, 1893, under more liberal state laws, a new holding company, the Long Island Traction Co. As soon as this was completed, the Long Island Traction Co. leased the Brooklyn Heights R.R. and through it, secured custody of the Brooklyn City R.R.

The horizon never looked more promising. The B.C.R.R. lease was to run for 999 years and the L.I.T.C., through the Brooklyn Height R.R. was to pay a 10% annual rental as a guarantee on the total capital stock. It was also to deposit four million dollars as a guarantee for the performance of the lease. The capital of the L.I.T.C was set at thirty million dollars. The traction company itself agreed to pay all fixed charges on the lines, maintain and run the road, and to sell three shares of stock of the par value of $100 each for $15 per share for each 10 shares of $10 parvalue Brooklyn City stock. This stock maneuver was not legal under New York State law, but the L.I.T.C. was not itself a railway company, and therefore not amenable to the laws of the State of New York.

Even the organization of the Long Island Traction Co. itself was questionable. It was owned and actively controlled by the original stockholders of the Brooklyn City R.R. Its entire $30 million in stock was issued at 15 cents on the dollar, illegal under New York State law; $27 million of this stock was offered to the holders of the outstanding $9 million of the Brooklyn City stock with the right of option to subscribe to and take $300 of the capital stock of the L.I.T.C. at 15 cents on the dollar. The remaining $3 million was sold in the market, also at 15 cents on the dollar. The proceeds of the sale of the $30 million realized 4-1/2 million and this was disposed of by taking $4 million to constitute the guarantee fund provided for in the lease agreement; the remainder went for general expenses.

The $4 million guarantee fund was duly deposited and was under no circumstances to be impaired, except that in the case of a failure on the part of the Brooklyn Heights R.R. to earn the 10% annual rental, it might, upon the maturity of any quarterly payment, draw upon the guarantee fund, but not in such a way as at any time to reduce it below $3-3/4 million. The $3 million capital stock and the $4 million in bonds remaining unissued in the treasury of the B.C.R.R. at the time that the lease was sold and the proceeds used to extend and electrify the lines.

In summary, the situation was this: the Long Island Traction Co., a Virginia corporation not organized for the purpose of constructing, owning and operating a railroad under New York State law, was instead owned by the holders of the Brooklyn City R.R. stock. They, in turn, through the L.I.T.C., owned and controlled the Brooklyn Heights R.R., which, in its turn, had secured a lease of all the properties of these very stockholders in the Brooklyn City R.R., on condition, however, that the lessee company should pay 10% to these shareholders in the Brooklyn City R.R. Co.

The effect of this operation was clearly to evade the laws of New York State so far as they restricted the issue of capital stock and the payment of taxes. It was obvious that the entire transaction was manipulated for three purposes:
1- To secure a guaranteed income under the terms of the lease.
2- To enable stockholders of the B.C.R.R. to continue to own and control these properties through another company which could issue capital stock at less than par value.
3- To avoid the corporation and tax laws of New York State.

The entire transaction promised very large returns when the properties became electrified, and great savings could be made in power, feed, cars and manpower. Other savings were to come from obtaining stock for below par value and avoiding taxation on the proposed new capital.

The plan failed. Without warning of any kind there developed in the winter and spring of 1893 a financial panic which had disastrous repercussions that the bankers could not have foreseen. All during the summer of 1893 the syndicate had been spending great sums of money tearing up the old horse car rails and relaying heavy 94lb. groove girder rail for electric operation; miles of trolley wire had been strung at high cost. Receipts on all the lines fell below expectations and the operation suddenly found itself in financial straits. The Long Island Traction Co., in order to pay the 10% dividend required on the Brooklyn City R.R. properties, had to dig into the $4 million guarantee fund; the whole $6 million gained by the sale of the B.C.R.R. unissued capital stock at the time of the lease had been swallowed up in electrifying the lines, and it was estimated that at least $3 million more was needed to pay debts and finish electrification. The B.H.R.R. even had to borrow $1 million in short term notes.

Before the depression of 1893 struck, the Long Island Traction Co. had been planning to sell unneeded real estate property of the B.C.R.R. and use the money to complete electrification. Because of the depressed market, they now feared to sell the assets. Meanwhile, earnings continued to decline in the face of continuing electrification bills, and the results were disastrous. The short term notes were issued to the stockholders to raise immediate cash to tide over the company in its crisis and they were to be redeemed by the sale of real estate and personal property of the railroad. Three million in such notes was issued and $1,850,000 was actually underwritten or subscribed at 80 cents on the dollar, the notes being guaranteed by pledging virtually everything which the B.H.R.R. and the L.I.T.C. owned. This whole procedure, managed by trustees with unlimited voting power, was certainly illegal and in violation of state law. In the end, these desperate measures failed to hold up the shaky structure; the L.I.T.C. failed to secure the money sought to be raised in anywhere near the full amount, and certain holders of the trust notes then made application to the U.S. Court in Virginia for a receivership. On March 26, 1895 this was granted. So ended the grandiose plans of the "traction ring" after reorganization emerged the Brooklyn Rapid Transit (BRT) system.

# 1895 Strike

The complicated financial maneuvres had not escaped scrutiny. The secrecy of the plans and the elaborate machinery set up to reap quick millions in profit created suspicion and condemnation by the media and public. The average motorman was paid only $2 for a long day's work, and could hardly be blamed for feeling resentful and distrustful of the traction companies. It was in this atmosphere that the great Brooklyn trolley strike of 1895 had its inception.

Contracts had existed with the union since 1886, and in 1887 it was renewed. The contract of 1888 was specific in fixing a 12 hour day. The contracts of 1890-1893 were made under the state Ten-Hour Law; specifing ten hours of running time within a 12 hour day. The company agreed to the principle of giving workers a voice in: fixing the number of trips; the proportion of trippers to regular cars; and the right of employees to arrange and approve time tables.

Negotiations had been on going since December 1894. The main point of contention was not pay, but the definition of a day's work. When the grievances presented by the union met with no sympathy on the part of the company, the union called for a strike vote.

When dawn broke on Monday, January 14, 1895, the trolley system of virtually all of Brooklyn lay paralyzed; 5000 men and 500 mechanics were out on strike.

The railroads immediatly started to hire replacement workers, which led to the strikers resorting to violence, rioting and wide spread damage to company property. The constant clashes with company workers and the police allowed the strikers to get out of control. The Mayor, fearing for public safety, on the 18th called out the National Guard. By the 20th there were 7,500 guardsmen on duty; they would stay until February 1st.

By the week of January 28th organized opposition had ended, and the strikers offered to settle on last year's terms but were turned down. The companies were getting more and more of their equipment in operation with replacement workers.

Several factors coming together had broken the back of the strike; the company's most powerful weapon was its army of replacement workers recruited from all parts of the country. Within seven days a sufficient force of motormen and conductors had been recruited to entirely replace the strikers on the key lines. When the union called off the strike on February 24th, it had long since lost the contest. Public exasperation at the interruption of service tended to overcome any sympathy for the strikers.

The strike was a shattering experience for both sides. The company lost fares, and suffered great damage to its equipment. The men lost their jobs; less than half were ever rehired, and then at entry level only.

## METROPOLITAN AVENUE IN THE '90'S

While the far-flung Brooklyn system was being transformed almost completely under the impact of extensive electrification, corporative reorganization and operating changes, the Metropolitan Ave. operation followed a path of evolution all its own, quite outside the Brooklyn City orbit. Unification, however, was in the air, and it was but a matter of time before the Metropolitan Ave. company, like so many other contemporary independents, should succumb to incorporation into a larger and more economic unit.

The initial impetus in the movement that was eventually to affect Metropolitan Ave. occurred in Jamaica in 1889. In June of that year the local owner of Brooklyn & Jamaica Road Co., operating the Jamaica Ave. horse cars, sold out his interest to Edward M. Field. In 1892 when his firm collapsed, the Jamaica Ave. trolley fell to the great Philadelphia banking firm of Drexel, Morgan & Co. This banking house had the benefit of long experience in managing railroads, and they invested large sums in modernizing and improving the Jamaica Ave. property. Because the trolley road terminated in East New York, and lacked an outlet to the East River ferries, the firm realized that Jamaica Ave. alone would never become the main artery of travel. The company, therefore, determined to secure an East River terminus and made overtures to the Brooklyn City R.R. to buy out the Fulton St. line, but were refused. They next negotiated with the Broadway R.R. Here again they were met with a refusal from the management, but some of the stockholders wavered. Secret negotiations were carried on all during the spring and summer of 1892; in October the sale was at last confirmed. Months later it was revealed that Drexel, Morgan & Co. had offered the stockholders $290 a share, an advance of 40 points over the market value, and they jumped at the chance.

In May 1892, Drexel, Morgan & Co. got a second chance at an East River terminal. Seven months before, the Metropolitan Ave. line, operated by its bondholders under the name of the Brooklyn, Bushwick & Queens County R.R., had gone into bankruptcy, and a receiver had been appointed on October 29, 1891. On Dec. 23, 1891 the Supreme Court ordered that the property of the company should be sold at public auction to satisfy a foreclosure judgement. On May 26, 1892 agents of Drexel, Morgan & Co. bought the road and reorganized it as the Broadway Ferry & Metropolitan Avenue R.R.

Thus within a year's time Drexel, Morgan & Co. had acquired a sizable railroad property totaling 44 miles. The Broadway R.R. owned besides its main line on Broadway from the East River to East New York, four branch routes: Reid Ave., Ralph Ave., Sumner Ave., and the Cypress Hills Extension on Fulton St., all horse car lines. The Jamaica Ave. line continued the Broadway route six miles further eastward to Jamaica, giving a through direct route from central Queens to the river. The Metropolitan Ave. line linked with the Broadway R.R. system at the Broadway Ferry, and serviced Williamsburgh and Bushwick.

On Nov. 24, 1893 Drexel, Morgan & Co. incorporated the Brooklyn, Queens County & Suburban R.R. Co. which first leased and then merged the three separate street railway properties into itself, cancelling all their stock. During the succeeding months the severe effects of the depression of 1893 began to make themselves felt, and the new company found it difficult to attract buyers for its securities. Late in 1893 the Brooklyn City R.R. agreed to invest two million dollars in the bonds of the Brooklyn, Queens County & Suburban on the condition that the entire capital stock of two million should accompany the bonds as a further consideration. In this way the entire capital stock of the Brooklyn, Queens County & Suburban R.R. was acquired and controlled by the Brooklyn Heights R.R., and ultimately, the Long Island Traction Company.

The Brooklyn, Queens County & Suburban R.R. Co. took formal possession of the properties in January 1894. At that time Jamaica Ave. was the only electric road and immediate steps were taken to electrify the others one by one. Since Metropolitan Ave. had the poorest record in earnings of any of the properties, it had to wait longest for modernization. Broadway, the trunk line of the system, was electrified on July 31, 1894; Ralph Avenue came next on Oct. 13, 1894; then Sumner Ave. on Nov. 18, 1894; Reid Avenue on Dec. 9, 1894; and finally the Cypress Hills Extension on Dec. 20, 1894.

Some time during the same year 1894, the Brooklyn, Queens County & Suburban management bought from Samuel Spencer, manager of the Railroad Department of Drexel, Morgan & Co., the bank's title to a plot of land on the east bank of Newtown Creek, bounded by Meserole St., Montrose Ave., and Varick Ave. This plot of ground had been acquired as a dock facility for the Broadway R.R. during the short time that the latter had been owned and operated by Drexel, Morgan & Co., and had been used for unloading barge-loads of paving stones, rails and general railroad supplies. To secure access to this railway dock, the B.Q.C. & S.R.R. utilized the route of one of its own constructed extensions, certificate for which had been filed with the Secretary of State a year before on March 13, 1893. This certificate authorized a single track from the corner of Metropolitan Ave. and Varick Ave. south down Varick Ave. to Flushing Ave. This extension or connection had very probably been originally motivated as a means of by-passing blocked bridges on Grand St. and Metropolitan Ave. by using Flushing Ave. as an alternate route. By the end of the year the single track had been installed in Varick Ave. as far down as Montrose Ave., where a loop track and several sidings serviced the dock. There was also an interchange track with the Bushwick Branch rails of the Long Island R.R. Between Stagg and Scholes Streets another siding serviced the dock facilities of the Barber Asphalt Co. For many years thereafter service cars of the Brooklyn Rapid Transit system made trips down this freight spur from time to time to load rails and paving stones delivered by barge. The Newtown Dock was used down to about 1920, after which it gradually fell into disuse, and was eventually dismantled and sold in 1929-30.

View of Newtown Docks, looking east from the canal, July 12, 1918. Note large piles of paving blocks on right. *Robert Presbrey collection.*

By the time the Metropolitan Ave. widening had been completed, the ownership of the old horse car property had passed to the Brooklyn, Queens County & Suburban R.R. The new railroad company applied in November 1893 for fresh extensions inside Queens which it hoped to build at the same time that Metropolitan Ave. itself should be electrified. The first extension requested was a northeasterly extension from the old terminus at the cemetery. Tracks were to be laid north up Dry Harbor Rd. (80th St.) to the Juniper Valley Rd., east along Juniper Valley to Woodhaven Blvd., and then east along a road now obliterated through the present Forest Hills to the old North Hempstead Plank Rd. (69th Rd.) and to Corona Ave., where connection would be made with the proposed Flushing trolley. A second extension was to continue on Metropolitan Ave. from Dry Harbor Rd. (80th St.) east to the Newtown-Jamaica Town line at about the present Lefferts Ave.

In the last days of March 1894 the company received permission from the Railroad Commission to electrify Metropolitan Ave. and the two proposed extensions. In the fall of 1894 the B.Q.C. & S.R.R. turned to the work of electrifying the long Metropolitan Ave. line. The first step in this extensive project was the installation of 94 lb. girder rail in place of the old worn horse car tracks between Kent Ave. and Bushwick Ave. Toward the end of the year wires were strung over the new rails. The strike of January 1895 seems not to have materially delayed the work; winter with its ice and snows would have put a stop to the work anyway. At the height of the strike about 2,000 ft. of trolley wire was cut down and carried away, but this was soon repaired. The work went on uninterruptedly and on Thursday, June 27, 1895, the first electric cars began operating along Metropolitan Ave. from Broadway Ferry to Bushwick Ave. to the city line and beyond horse cars continued in use. It is interesting to note that Metropolitan Ave. was the last of all the lines in Brooklyn to be electrified; only the very short Hunter's Point shuttle continued to use horses and these finally went in 1900. The horse cars had dominated Brooklyn transportation for 40 years; the trolley was now supreme.

At the same time that electrification was under way, the company reduced the fare between Niederstein's Hotel (69th St.) and Broadway Ferry from 8 cents to 5 cents; all the horse cars were run through from Bushwick Ave. to 69th St. instead of turning back at the creek or the Onderdonk Ave. stables.

The authorities in Queens County had mixed feelings on the matter of electrifying the Queens end of the line. Although they were delighted at the prospect of modern transportation, they were not happy at seeing Metropolitan Ave. torn up all over again to lay rails.

Car in front of *Niederstein's Resturant*, a landmark in Middle Village, 1947. The facade has since been modernized. (69th St.)

The march of progress could not long be stayed. In August 1895 the company began relaying the rails from the Newtown Creek bridge to Metropolitan Park at Flushing Ave. with T rail; the local residents were furious, for T rail was notorious for obstructing roads and overturning wagons. Possibly because of the very vocal opposition, or because of lack of capital, nothing further was done for the year.

In the spring of 1896 the project was resumed. On March 23rd the work of laying tracks and setting up trolley poles for the new electric road was again begun, and rapidly pushed forward eastward from the city line. By April 30th the second segment of the electrification had opened, the trolley going as far as Bushwick Junction station (Fresh Pond Rd.). The good spring weather made for rapid progress in both track laying and wire stringing. By May 9th or 10th a third section was opened to trolley operation, this time the segment from Fresh Pond Rd. to Neiderstein's Hotel at 69th St. Within one week the final section from 69th St. to St. John's Cemetery was opened on or about May 16, 1896. At the same time the Brooklyn, Queens County & Suburban abolished the old fare structure; henceforth a single 5 cent fare took the passenger the whole distance from Broadway Ferry to the cemetery without an extra 3 cent charge and without a change of cars.

It seems likely that at this time the short segment of line north into Dry Harbor Rd. (80th St.) was built, 1,061 ft. or .2 mile, either as a storage space for extra cars on busy cemetery visiting days, or as a legal device to hold the Dry Harbor Rd. franchise. It was but a single track and cars did not ordinarily turn onto it.

With the opening of electric service through the full length of Metropolitan Ave., the long series of changes in ownership, rolling stock, and operation comes to an end, and the trolley operation settles down to a long period of peaceful and generally uneventful routine down to the days of World War I.

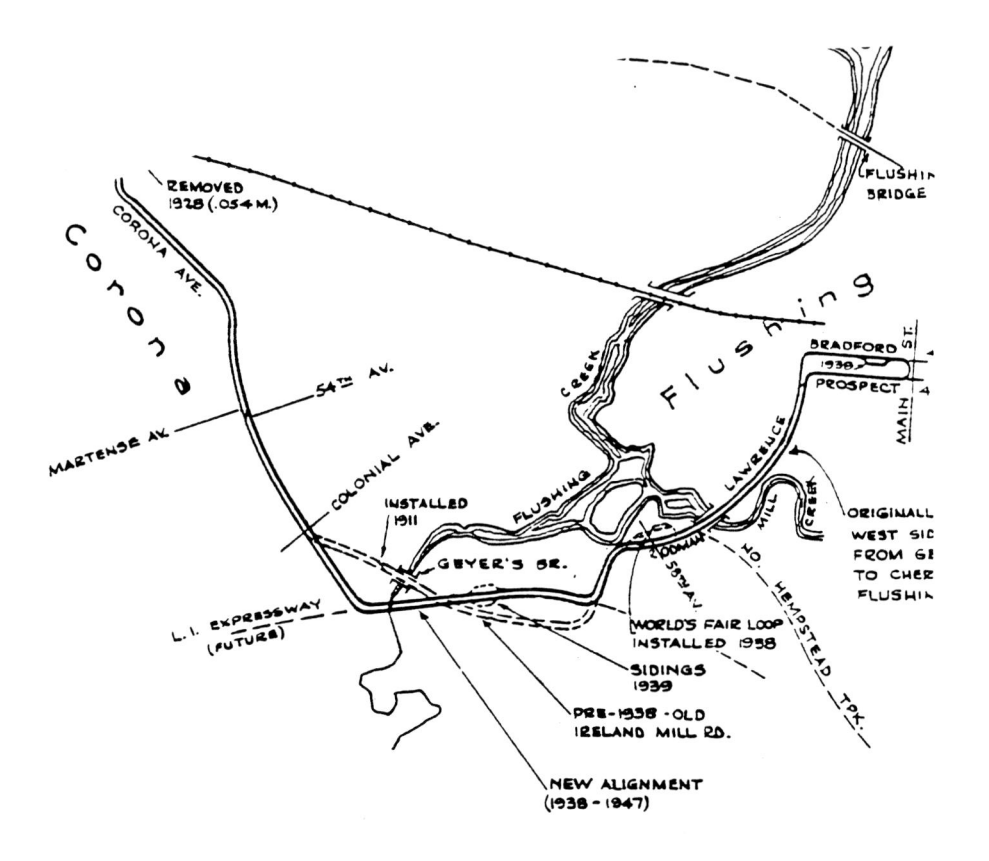

# THE BROOKLYN CITY RAILROAD REACHES FLUSHING

When the Brooklyn City R.R. embarked upon its big program of trolley extension northeast from Newtown Village (Elmhurst) in the early '90's, there was but one large population center of any consequence worth building to - the old town of Flushing. This stately old town of 12,000 inhabitants with its many mansions, majestic trees and beautiful suburbs originated a fairly heavy railroad traffic and supported a small street railway line of its own. No traction system had as yet connected Flushing with the city and what rail travel there was remained a monopoly of the Long Island R.R.

When the Brooklyn City R.R. made its decision to build to North Beach, it was decided at the same time to push on to Flushing. The directors were convinced that the proposed trolley would not only attract to itself much of the lucrative traffic now monopolized by the L.I.R.R., but would also open up to Flushingites the big downtown shopping centres along Grand St. and Fulton St. The great differential in fare alone was considered certain to attract much of the Flushing trade and direct travel from New York to lower Brooklyn, 10 cents on the trolley against 15 cents on the railroad.

The first move in the direction of building the Flushing extension was taken in the fall of 1893 when the Brooklyn City R.R. applied to the Highway Commissioners of the Town of Newtown for a double track extension along Corona Ave. from Junction Ave. to Flushing Creek. The request was granted on October 31, 1893. Three months later in January 1894 they applied to the Town of Flushing to continue the proposed route from Flushing Creek along Strong's Causeway, Ireland Mill Rd. and Lawrence Ave. to the village boundary. At this time only two roads entered Flushing: Jackson Ave. on the north and Strong's Causeway on the south. It was decided to adopt the southern road for several reasons; no crossing of the L.I.R.R. tracks would be required; the village of Corona with 2,900 inhabitants and Corona Heights with 500 would originate some traffic along the route; finally, possible heavy future holiday traffic might result from the fact that the new line would pass in front of the proposed site of the new Cedar Grove Cemetery.

The prospect of a new trolley line through this empty and desolate area was welcomed. The consents of Corona Ave. property owners were quickly obtained, as there were scarcely any houses in the two mile stretch from Corona station to the Flushing village line. On March 17, 1894 approval was given by Flushing; but three conditions were set:

44

The railroad must contribute $2,000 for repairing Strong's bridge.
It must contribute half the cost, not to exceed $5,000, of filling in the causeway to a width of 40 ft. and raising it 3 ft..
That a block pavement be used instead of cobble stones.
The matter then went to the village trustees for approval.

The trustees were in favor of letting the cars run to, but not through the town, but the railroad's representatives warned that the company would not invest its money under such conditions. On May 19th the trustees reported the application back to the company denying it the use of Main St. or Bradford Ave. (41 Ave.) and suggesting that Bradford and Lawrence Avenues be made the terminal, or that the company should operate over the tracks of the Flushing and College Point line through the village. This the Brooklyn City refused. Due to public pressure the board reversed itself on October 30, 1894, and agreed to the Brooklyn City's terms. The company was required to begin the work in a year and to complete the work within another year; the fare was set at 5 cents within the village limits and 10 cents to downtown Brooklyn.

For the next year nothing was done on the Flushing project. The company's attention was absorbed by the disastrous strike and riots of January 1895 and every cent was needed to rehabilitate the damaged rolling stock and overhead wires. Then on March 26th the Long Island Traction Co. went into receivership, and the prospect of extension faded. But in November 1895 a letter was received by the Town of Flushing containing the road's check for $2,500 as the company's portion of the repairs to Strong's Causeway. In October the Town of Newtown completed its half of the Causeway improvement at an expense of $9.090 and received a check for $2,500 from the Brooklyn City R.R.

The route the Brooklyn City chose was at that time one of the least settled in Queens and the least attractive to settlement. From Junction Ave. the route passed along what was then known as Newtown Ave. then along Corona Ave. to Strong's Causeway, then along the causeway and finally along Ireland Mill Rd. to Lawrence Ave. Today Newtown Ave. and Corona Ave. have become Corona Ave. and most of Strong's Causeway is part of the Long Island Expressway; Ireland Mill Rd. is now College Point Blvd.

When the Brooklyn City R.R. arrived on the scene in 1895, ready to lay tracks along the causeway, their engineers discovered that the road had been sinking for several years and still was, and that the salt meadow was almost like quicksand. When soundings of the roadbed were made, a hard foundation was found to be 45 to 60 ft. down.

Car No.1817 of the Metropolitan Ave. line, a typical 10-bench open used in summer before WW I.

While the commissioners of both towns were meeting on February 11, 1896 to settle the matter of strengthening Strong's Bridge for the trolleys they were informed that the causeway and bridge had just subsided ten feet. A new bridge was recommended, and there being no alternative, was authorized on March 27th.

Meanwhile the Brooklyn City R.R. began active construction in April under the direction of William T. Cameron, who had built the Steinway R.R. Cameron directed a force of 200 men and they made such excellent progress that by May the northbound track was completed as far as the causeway bridge. Nine-inch Johnson girder rail was used, 32 ft. long with chains 7 ft 6 in. apart, spiked to pine ties every 2-1/2 ft.; the space between the rails was covered with heavy plank. Tubular iron piles held the trolley wire.

The work proceeded energetically all through the spring and summer, and by the end of August the double track had been practically completed all the way to the Flushing village line.

Looking west along Strong's Causeway over the meadows just before the 1939 World's Fair with Corona in the distance; this is now the Long Island Expressway, January 1937. *Alfred Seible* photo.

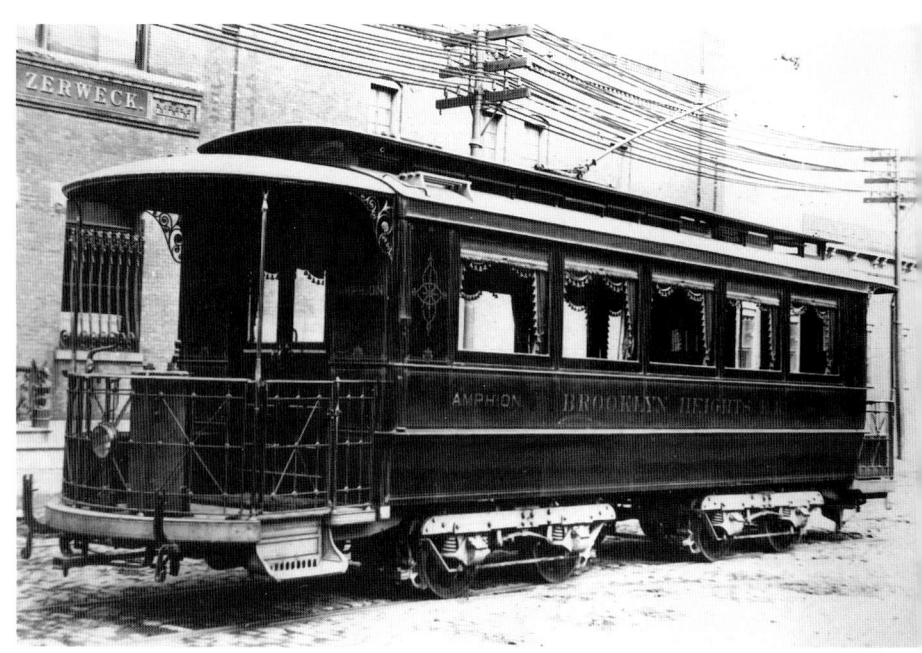

Parlor cars were a luxury feature on the BRT lines in the 1890's, the street car's answer to such cars on steam railroads. The names Amphion, Montauk and Columbia were taken from popular Brooklyn theatres. Eventually all three cars were rebuilt into everyday trolley cars.

Strong's Bridge remained the only gap in the line. The new bridge was scheduled to open on September 1, 1896. When completed and tested it was discovered that a 3 foot gap yawned between the bridge and the abutment. After a few days the one approach was extended to cover the gap. The new bridge, built by the Berlin Bridge Co., was 135 ft. long and 30 ft. wide. The road began laying tracks on the bridge to close the gap in the now nearly completed line. By October 8th the work was nearly done, and the company made an agreement with the highway board to pay $2,000 toward the cost of the bridge, to provide an extra number of electric lights, and to keep the planking and approaches in repair.

On Saturday October 24, 1896, the new trolley line was formally opened. At 12 noon President Rossiter with other officials of the road and the city left City Hall in Brooklyn in the parlorcar "Columbia" and journeyed out to Flushing. In Flushing they met five other cars, filled with town officials and locally prominent people. The parlor cars "Montauk" and "Amphion" followed closely behind the "Columbia", and three of the newest passenger cars, Nos. 742, 743 & 748, brought up the rear. The fact that this new line now connected Flushing directly with Brooklyn for the first time was frequently emphasized on the trip. President Rossiter announced that special parlor car service for the convenience of ladies desiring to shop in

46

Brooklyn would be instituted immediately on Tuesdays and Fridays of each week, making two trips a day at 9:30 a.m. and 2:00 p.m. The parlor cars made no stops and the trip was to take exactly one hour, the fare being 20 cents one way or 35 cents round trip. Regular service opened the next day. The Flushing Ave. line was extended from Maspeth Depot and ran through from the Fulton Ferry to Flushing for a 10 cent fare and under 20 minute headway. With the completion of the extension to Flushing the Brooklyn trolley system had expanded to its fullest limits in Queens County, and many years would pass before any new construction would be attempted. The next years were a period of consolidating gains, a period of development and settlement of the vast new areas opened to rapid transit for the first time.

**Luxurious interior of the Parlor Car *Columbia* as seen in a Brill photo of 1895.** *Edward Watson collection*

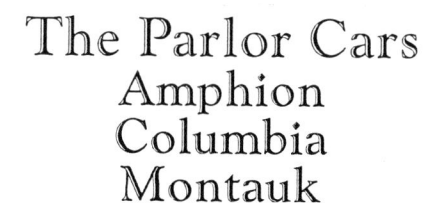

The Parlor Cars
Amphion
Columbia
Montauk

# RECOVERY & EXPANSION 1895-1900

As soon as the disastrous trolley strike of 1895 had passed, the company lost no time in rehabilitating the system. Months passed before traffic returned to its old level; receipts were in the neighborhood of $1,500 a day less than the year before.

A determined effort was made to raise the caliber of men employed, and to cultivate an esprit-de-corps that would insure against any further disruptions. All new conductors hired had to be bonded with a casualty company in New York. Formerly, a private bondsman was taken, but it was found that when the conductor absconded with a couple of trip collections, the bondsman ended up poorer than the man who "knocked down" $10. This new bonding meant the close scrutiny of a man's record, and permanent loss of employment for dishonesty.

On August 1, 1895 an order went into effect requiring all motormen and conductors to wear uniforms. These cost $9.25 each, and consisted of trousers and coat of Middlesex blue, and a uniform blue cap similar to yachting caps of the time. There were two sets of buttons, one of brass while on duty, the other of bone for off-duty. Three years later the company had fully recovered and was making money, and in 1898 all conductors and motormen who had put in three years of service since the strike received increases in salary.

Car No 4573 on Flushing Ave., looking west at the old Wyckoff farm house at 1325 Flushing Ave., built in 1719. It was the home of the ex-president of the Grand St. & Newtown R.R., the family was very prominent in old Bushwick. August 23, 1948. *Robert Presbrey collection.*

The close of the year 1895 saw the final reorganization of the Long Island Traction Co. On March 26, 1895 this giant company had gone into receivership under the combined blows of excessive stock manipulation, depression, and the crushing effects of a strike. The entire corporate structure was aired in the courts, and a reorganization that protected the rights of all parties was adopted. A new holding company was formed, the Brooklyn Rapid Transit (BRT), to assume the assets on January 18, 1896. All the old underlying leases were assigned to it, and on January 24, 1896 the transfer went into effect. So well did the court do its work, and so stable was the financial structure set up, that the B.R.T., as it came to be familiarly called, survived intact for the next quarter century.

The B.R.T., on taking over the management of its vast properties, made commendable efforts to keep up with the times by adapting its routes and services to the requirements of a population that was increasing enormously every year, and expanding eastward at an unprecedented rate. In the fall of 1895 and spring of 1896 the company came under repeated fire in Elmhurst and Corona because of poor service. Apparently little attention was paid to this remote corner of the system and headways stretched to 40 minutes and one hour at the Corona terminus. In Newtown after a half hour wait, two cars often came along together. The management at Maspeth was little interested in the outer end of the line; often the Corona car was unmarked, and after riders had hopefully boarded one assuming it to be the correct trolley, a different one would start down the tracks and leave them stranded. People traveling from Brooklyn at night ran a greater risk; no official at Maspeth could be found to tell them when the last car to Corona was scheduled, or even if it would run at all. After many complaints, there was a change of personnel at Maspeth Depot and things improved almost overnight. As of July 1, 1895, all cars from Newtown ran through to the ferry, and from the ferry every third car ran through to Newtown.

To improve service beyond the point of just shortening headways, several route changes were tried as experiments, some of which later became permanent and surived to the end of trolley service. On August 11, 1895, a new crosstown line was started, from Meeker Ave. at Penny Bridge, running through Humboldt, Grand, Flushing, Washington and Myrtle Avenues to City Hall. In effect it was an extension of the old Meeker Ave. line of the Grand St. & Newtown R.R. The advantage of this new route, however, lay in the fact that people could now travel from Prospect Park or 65th St. Brooklyn to Corona or North Beach for two fares instead of three, transfers being issued at Grand and Humboldt for the first time.

The B.R.T. now turned its attention to the Flushing Ave. and Fresh Pond lines on which tracks had been laid in August and May 1893 respectively, but never used due to refusal of the

L.I.R.R. to permit crossings at grade. New negotiations were entered into, and at length an agreement was reached. The B.R.T. at the absolute insistence of the L.I.R.R. adopted the block signal system at each grade crossing. According to the agreement the trolley company assumed the expense of putting in the signals, while the L.I.R.R. would operate them. The operator sat in a tower beside the L.I.R.R. tracks, a set of wires connected him with the two semaphores on either side of the crossing. The semaphores were always set at danger, and the motorman always brought his car to a stop, the tower operator observing this, then changed the signal to "all clear".

In August 1899 further precautions were taken. The L.I.R.R. installed crossing gates across the avenue, and in addition to a signalman, a flagman was added. The conductor had to stop his car 50 ft. from the crossing, walk ahead, and flag his car across.

Part of the reason driving the B.R.T. to open the two blocked lines was the threat of a lawsuit to cancel the franchises along Flushing Ave. and Fresh Pond Rd., on the grounds of non-operation. On January 22, 1896 the company ran test cars over both routes up to each of the blocked crossings and back to test the rails and overhead and also to hold the franchise. Finally on April 1, 1896 the Flushing Ave. line was opened through to Maspeth Depot and through cars began running between the barns and Brooklyn Bridge. On the same day the Crosstown-Meeker line was terminated, and the old Grand-Meeker service restored. Transfers were given at Graham Ave. for those riders desiring to use the former crosstown route, and the transfer point at Grand and Humboldt was discontinued. With the coming of spring the Flushing Ave. line was extented through to North Beach, and the construction of a loop to lay up cars at the amusement site was undertaken.

On Thursday June 20, 1896 the B.R.T. announced the opening of the Fresh Pond line; cars began at the Ridgewood depot at Myrtle and Palmetto St., continued along the Lutheran line to Fresh Pond Rd.; then along Fresh Pond Rd., Grand St. and Junction Ave. to Bowery Bay. This was the first time service had been possible along Fresh Pond Rd. and the route formed the beginning of the later Flushing-Ridgewood route.

On Saturday October 24, 1896, the Flushing Ave. line was extended to Flushing and the Flushing Ave. cars stopped running to North Beach, leaving that service to the newly opened Fresh Pond line. On Saturday, January 16, 1897, another important route change was made by inauguration of the Grand & Ridgewood line. The new line began at the Grand St. Ferry and ran along Grand, Meserole, Bushwick, Flushing, Knickerbocker and Myrtle Avenues to the Ridgewood Depot. By the late 90's retail trade began moving away from Grand St. and over to Broadway and the line lost traffic gradually from the day it

Myrtle Ave. car #4557 as een in an equipment view. *Edward Watson* photo.

started. As a result, on January 30, 1899, the Grand & Ridgewood line was closed, and in its place the Flushing-Knickerbocker line was created, using the two streets named between Park Row and Ridgewood Depot. In other words, as of January 30th, three lines of cars ran along Flushing Ave. : Flushing-Knickerbocker, Flushing to Corona, and Flushing Ave. to Flushing.

It was during the five year period, 1895-1900, that extensive improvements took place in rolling stock. At the end of the strike large numbers of cars had been damaged, and the remainder were electrified horse cars, too light and too small to carry the increasing passenger loads. Between 1895 and 1899 the entire fleet was renewed with the purchase of about 700 new cars from several different builders. The acquisition of this large fleet enabled the B.R.T. to retire the old electrified horse cars and to give faster, more frequent service to a greater volume of passengers.

In December 1897 the B.R.T. changed the color of its cars from bottle green to the familiar red and yellow that endured until the city aquired the trolley properties. On August 17th they began the practice of placing red lanterns on the rear of the suburban cars. Experience had shown that when cars ran on under a minute headway at night, and the trolley pole jumped the wire, the cars were left in total darkness.. By using the red lanterns rear-end collisions were cut to a minimum. This improvement was followed by a change in the route signs, instead of the large dashboard signs, cars were equipped with a wooden block sign on the hood, which could be revolved to show four possible destinations, at night the signs on the deck roof indicated routes.

Fresh Pond Rd. looking north from the Long Island R.R. tracks at Metropolitan Ave., March 25, 1915. *Robert Presbrey collection.*

Most noteworthy of all the new rolling stock that appeared in the 90's were the parlor cars or palace cars for private use. The idea of luxurious street cars offering drawing room comforts for premium fares was not a new one, the Third Avenue R.R. in New York operated a palace car service as early as 1870. It was in the 90's, however, the this luxury reached full flower, and a varied development that brought it within the means of the masses as well as the wealthy.

It was the materialistic social climate of the 90's that brought the parlor car into its own. It was an age of elegance, an age that admired the opulence and the lush magnificence to be seen in the houses of a thousand tycoons, all newly rich and eager to display that fact as publicly as possible. The traction tycoons of the day showed the same love of ostentation. To demonstrate the growing size and power of their street railways, they copied many of the trappings of the railroad magnates, and the private car was one of the most visible symbols of affluence and position. On many roads the president and board of directors alone rode the parlor cars; in Brooklyn the palace car from the beginning was a more democratic affair. Anyone could ride it who was willing to pay the extra fare.

In 1894 the Brooklyn City R.R. placed at the disposal of the "carriage trade" segment of its patrons two handsomely furnished trolleys, the "Amphion" and the "Montauk", names of two of the largest downtown theatres of the day. A third parlor car, the "Columbia", followed in 1895. All three were glittering creations of the car-builders art; their exteriors sported five large picture windows set off by the deep finish of the car body, which was rubbed to a high polish, and decorated with gold lettering and scroll work. The car platforms resembled railroad observation cars, being wider than usual, fitted for cushioned seats and surrounded by ornamental iron grill work. The interior boasted a carpet running the full length of the car, and eight wicker chairs on each side, each with a velvet cushion. At the windows were heavy plush drapes and ornamental scroll-work coat hooks. The ceiling was paneled with cabinet woods decorated with garlands, and a colonial secretary fitted to dispense both books and refreshments had been built into each corner. A uniformed waiter and a porter catered to the comfort of the passengers. All this magnificence could be enjoyed for five times the usual fare-only 25 cents.

All three, the "Amphion", "Montauk" and the "Columbia", passed many of their best years in Queens County. On October 24, 1896, the three cars rode in procession to Flushing for the formal opening of the Flushing extension. The prominent people of the community filled the cars and a complete lunch was served. Beginning the next day, and for the next three years the parlor cars became a regular institution on the Flushing line. After Brooklyn, Flushing was the next largest town on the island, and contained many wealthy and prominent people. It was to cater to this trade and to divert it from New York to Brooklyn that the B.R.T. set up the regular weekly parlor car service. On every Tuesday and Friday two parlor cars ran between Flushing and City Hall, Brooklyn, for the convenience of ladies wishing to shop downtown. The cars made no intermediate stops and made the trip in an hour, the fare was 20 cents one way and 35 cents round trip.

The parlor car service became quite fashionable and so numerous were the requests to extend this service to connect with the Brooklyn theatres that the company arranged for additional cars. On December 9, 1896 and each Wednesday thereafter the residents of any of the towns along the line were able to attend either matinee or evening performances of any Brooklyn theatre.

On October 4, 1897 the parlor car service was resumed between Flushing and the ferry. Three trips a week were scheduled for Monday, Wednesday and Saturday, and three cars on each day, an increase over the previous season. Cars left Flushing at 9:45 a.m., 1:00 and 3:15 p.m., returning cars left City Hall at 11:45 a.m., 2:30 and 5:15 p.m. The cars were still getting liberal patronage, especially for the theatres; the fare was still 35 cents including the coupon for a chair.

Open bench illuminated excursion car, first used August 17, 1895, at Ridgewood Park 1896. *Edward Watson collection.*

Open bench illuminated excursion car, first used August 17, 1895, at Ridgewood Park 1896. *Vincent F. Seyfried collection.*

Even more popular during this period than the parlor cars were the excursion trolleys. Only the more well to do could aspire to a parlor car ride, but an excursion car was within the means of all. The excursion car differed from the parlor car in that it catered to a sizable group rather than a private party. It was invariably an open car, and so could accommodate from 72 to 90 people. At first there was only the ordinary rolling stock to offer; when these slow, small cars proved inadequate, the company used the larger 12 bench steam coaches recently displaced from the Ft. Hamilton line, and glamourized them for excursion use. Two strings of colored light bulbs were strung the length of the letterboard, and diamond-shaped patterns of bulbs decorated each dashboard. The whole roof was studded with lights. Instead of curtains, festoons of red, white and blue bunting hung at the sides, and the iron seat bases were draped over with white hangings. Six of these bird-of paradise cars were turned out in July 1895, numbered in the 3200 series, and all six ran in procession through the streets for the first time on August 7th to advertise the new service. A morning outing cost $10, afternoon $15 and evening $20. The cars would arrive at any designated spot at any time, and there was a large choice of destinations.

The suburban Queens routes offered picnic grounds, beer halls, Schuetzen Parks and North Beach. In Brooklyn you could vist Ulmer Park, Coney Island, Manhattan Beach, Canarsie, Far Rockaway, and the races at Sheepshead Bay. The first recorded excursion in Queens, advertised as "the latest novelty for outings", took place on August 21, 1895, and ran to Ulmer Park and back. Men paid $1 and ladies 75 cents. Not long after, Lutheran Cemetery employees went on outing. Within a year the trolley party idea really caught on. In July 1896 one of the largest trolley parties on record passed through Newtown village; it consisted of 14 illuminated cars, carrying over 750 people to North Beach. By 1898 the parties had become common place. The trolley party retained its popularity for a decade; only with the advent of the automobile touring car did they die off.

The 90's witnessed the flowering not only of the parlor car and excursion car business, but also the organization and growth of the trolley express and the trolley mail. In an age when the trolley was the fastest form of local transportation, the idea of entrusting packages and mail to the traction company seemed sensible and practical. In April 1896 the National Express Co. concluded an agreement with the B.R.T. for the shipment of express goods by trolley all over Brooklyn and Queens. The total number of express cars contemplated was 6, and their operation would not interfere with the 1,100 passenger cars in use carrying 500,000 passengers a day. Each express car would make 4 or 5 trips daily. On June 15, 1896 the new express service began; one of the routes ran from the Broadway Ferry through Grand St. to the Corona post office, which was made the station for the express company. From here delivery wagons received and delivered goods for the villages of Corona, Newtown, Maspeth and North Beach.

B.C.R.R. National Express car No 24 on September 12, 1899; it later was renumber to No141 in 1904 and finally No9551 in 1906. *Edward Watson collection.*

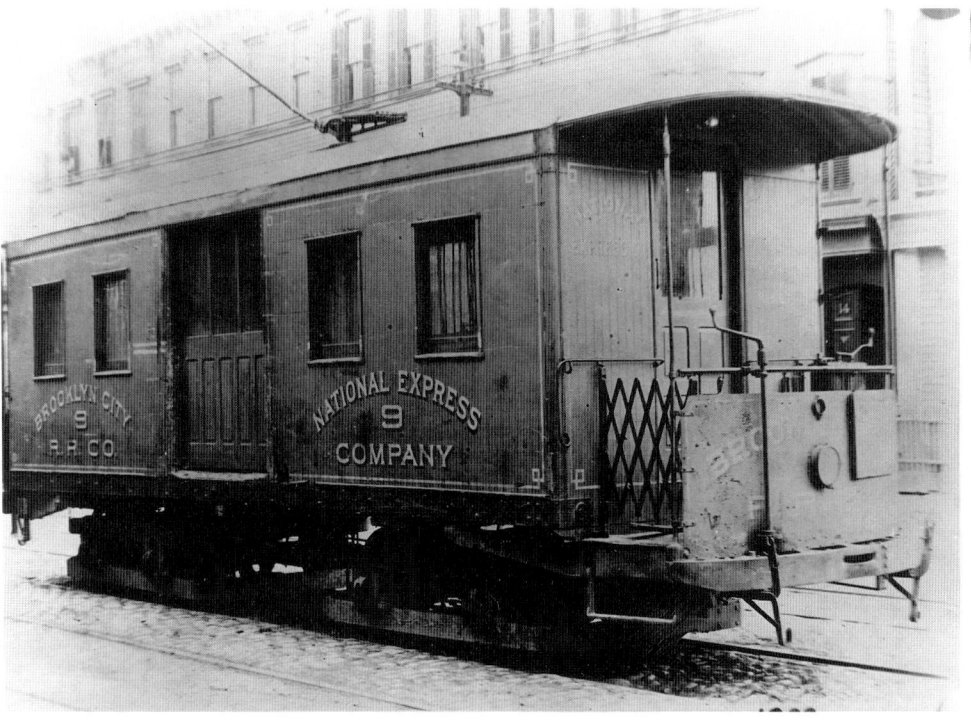

B.C.R.R. National Express Co. car No 9, December 1899. The car was renumbered several timesto; No29 in 1900, No146 in 1904 & No9556 in 1906. *Edward Watson collection.*

On June 22, 1896 the National Express Co. opened a large office adjoining the car barn at Manhattan Ave. and Box St. for the Greenpoint-Williamsburgh srevice. Thirty depots in all were opened, the central one being located at the foot of Broadway near the ferry. Other stations were at Fulton Ferry and at the outer terminals of the line. Besides the depots there were almost 100 call stations. The trolley cars first used in this service were eight small single truck cars numbered 1-8, built by Stephenson in 1895. They had four barred windows on each side, and a door in the center. In 1897 two double truck express cars #9 & 10 were bought from Brill. All cars were painted dark blue and carried the legend "Brooklyn City R.R. Co." and "National Express Company". In 1898 the cars were renumbered cars #1-8 to #21-28, and in 1904 renumbered all 10 cars to #138-147.

To stimulate the express business as much as possible, the B.R.T. invited the owners, supervisors, and managers of all the large retail stores in the downtown area for an excursion aboard the parlor car "Columbia" to familiarize them with the extensive territory covered by the cars, and the speed and ease of delivery of packages.

52

The trolley express business was very successful from the beginning and carried a large amount of express matter. For 10 years the trolley express continued to operate over the whole B.R.T. system until the competition from the first auto trucks began to be felt. The National Express Co. was sold in 1905 to the American Express Co. In December 1908 the American Express Co. posted public notices in all its offices, that because the B.R.T refused to lower its rental, all trolley express service would be discontinued as of January 1, 1909. The heavy freight business involving the use and interchange of standard freight cars went right on in South Brooklyn over the Culver, Sea Beach and West End tracks. On July 30, 1903 the B.R.T. set up a subsidiary called the American Railway Traffic Co. and this in 1910 was sold to the South Brooklyn Rwy. which has continued the freight business to the present.

Hardly less novel than the express service was the trolley mail. The inspiration to use street cars as adjuncts of the postal system was not original to Brooklyn, the idea was first tried successfully in St. Louis. Brooklyn was a much larger city than St. Louis and with a far larger trolley network, and offered even greater possibilities. The Atlantic Ave. R.R. Co. was the first to adopt trolley mail in Brooklyn, and on June 12, 1894 concluded a contract with the Post Office to carry mail in a special white car from the downtown post office to the city line at 36th St. The service opened on August 4th over Fifth and Atlantic Avenues, and to Coney Island over the West End tracks.

The Brooklyn City R.R. was next to make an agreement; on December 20, 1894 a contract was signed to carry mail from the General Post Office to Flatbush and Flatlands, on January 7, 1895 the first runs were made. On April 9th trolley cars began carrying the mails along Third Ave., Brooklyn, to Ft. Hamilton. As the service gradually increased, it became apparent that the small single-truck passenger cars were unequal to the traffic, and it was decided that new cars, especially adapted to carrying and processing mail en route should be ordered. In December 5 new mail cars were delivered from J.G. Brill Co., and promptly fitted and tested for service. In January 1896 two additional cars arrived. In all there were seven cars, numbered 1-7; they were painted white and divided into both mail and regular passenger compartments.

In April 1897 permission was granted to open a suburban mail route along Grand St. and Corona Ave. out to Flushing, servicing Flushing and Maspeth Post Offices and branch sub-offices in Corona,, and Newtown, Metropolitan, the Queens side of Grand St. Where it had taken a letter 1 hour to travel from Newtown to downtown Brooklyn, it now took 45 minutes. The car made 4 trips a day and handled all mail addressed to Brooklyn.

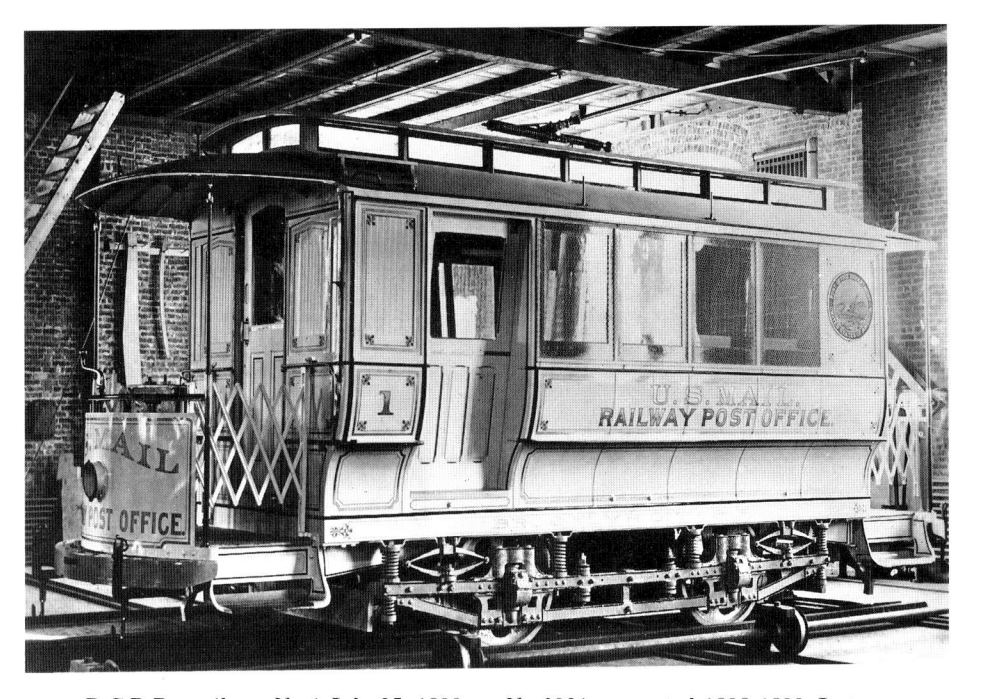

B.C.R.R. mail car No 1 July 25, 1899, ex No 3921 converted 1898-1899. Later renumbered to No 215 in 1900, and again to No 9602 in 1906.; scrapped in 1921. *Edward Watson collection.*

On October 13, 1898 the Brooklyn-Flushing service was curtailed; thereafter R.P.O. trolleys brought mail to Station A at Broadway and Flushing Ave. only, where a regular passenger car carried the pouch the rest of the way to Flushing.

Within a year or two it became evident that the combination mail cars were not successful. Passengers complained when the mail crew stopped for pickups, and mail crews fretted at the delays in picking up and discharging passengers. To please everyone, all seven mail cars were converted for passenger only service, and replaced with seven old remodeled single truck cars.

During the 1900-1910 period passenger loads increased enormously, and it was inevitable that at certain times and places, the mail cars would interfere with the quick passage of the passenger cars. These delays became an increasing source of friction between the B.R.T.'s operating department and the Post Office. On January 6, 1913 the B.R.T. annnounced that no more closed pouch mail would be handled on its regular passenger cars. Then in March the mail service between Station A and Flatbush was ended. The Post Office had been making increasing use of wagons, and it became clear that both parties

Car No. 4105 of the Grand St. line on the Queens side of Newtown Creek Bridge, the bridge has swung open to let a boat pass.

wished to discontinue the Railway Post Office service. The end was not long in coming; on August 31, 1914 the cars made their last trip.

In the spring of 1898 many of the downtown Brooklyn lines began using the newly completed tracks over the Brooklyn Bridge to Park Row. By using the Flushing Ave. cars from Maspeth, residents of Newtown, Maspeth and Corona could now reach lower New York for a 5 cent fare.

## THE NORTH SIDE LINES - 1900-1917

Side by side with the changing patterns in local transportation were the slow alterations of ethnic groups in northern Brooklyn and the western fringes of Queens. Immigration of new groups into the area was not the only reason for the shifts in population. Two other major influences were the pollution of Newtown Creek by rising industries, and the opening of the Williamsburgh Bridge.

The pollution of Newtown Creek became a menace, and by 1900 the very name Newtown became associated in the public mind with noxious stenches, that in summer drifted over the city making life miserable for the inhabitants. In Queens a large real estate firm found that the name Newtown, even though applying to the village 3 miles away had become one in the public mind with the creek and tended to make homes unsalable. The firm negotiated with the postal authorities to change the name of the 250 year old village. In the fall of 1896 Newtown was officially changed to Elmhurst. Today the name Newtown is only a memory, though preserved in two places, Newtown High School in Corona and the IND subway station at Grand St.

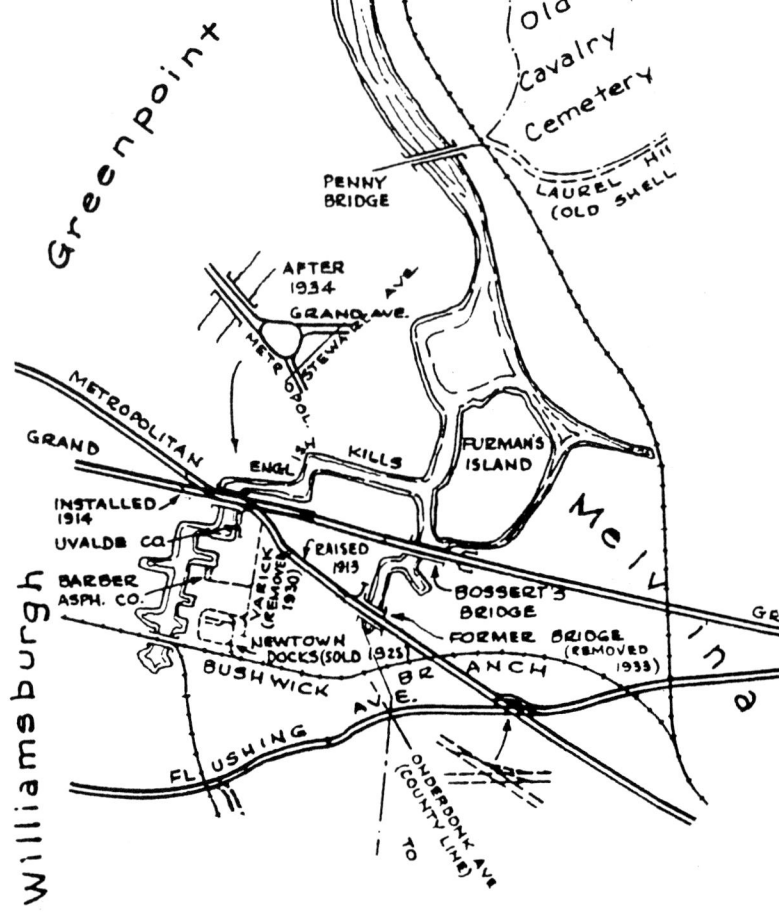

Far more influential than Newtown Creek in altering the population complexion and economic pattern of Williamsburgh was the opening of the Williamsburgh Bridge from Grand St., Manhattan, to Broadway, Brooklyn. Authorized and approved 1895, construction was begun on Oct. 28, 1896 and completed Dec. 19, 1903. A large plaza was carved out of former residential

54

streets in the square bounded by Havemeyer, South 4th Sts., Driggs Ave. and Broadway, and a large trolley terminal consisting of many loops and access tracks was constructed. The Allied Boards of Trade particularly the Grand St. group, alarmed at the further loss of retail trade, to New York, bitterly fought to keep the B.R.T. car lines from carrying passengers away from the old Brooklyn terminals to a new Manhattan terminal, but the courts failed to sustain them.

Beginning Nov. 3, 1904 cars of the Broadway, Reid, Franklin, Hamburg, Nostrand, Grand and Bushwick lines began to use the new bridge.

The effects of this new traffic artery were profound. The Broadway and Grand St. ferries, once the focal points of the densest traffic, declined rapidly, fewer and fewer persons continued riding the old ferries. Downtown Broadway, which had enjoyed a brief boom in retail business since about 1895, again began to decline, lower Grand St., once the busiest business center of north Brooklyn, rapidly went into eclipse through the diversion of retail trade over the bridge to Manhattan. The decline of lower Grand St. was further accelerated by the opening of the Grand St. Extension, a cut-off that carried Grand St. in a straight line from Union Ave. to Bridge Plaza. When this had first been proposed in 1898, the very suggestion had aroused a storm of protest; merchants pointed out that lower Grand St. would become a backwater, and that half a dozen residential streets would be chopped through once the new Williamsburgh Bridge was opened; their protest availed nothing, and the Grand St. Extension was cut through, sealing the doom of the old business section.

The changing economic and social conditions may serve to explain at least in part two phenomena of the early 20th century, the slow but steady decline of the B.R.T. lines in Williamsburgh and Bushwick, and the corresponding growth and heavy patronage of the once-suburban routes in Queens County. After 1898, census statistics for the individual villages of Queens are rare, but the list of December 1898 survives, and is extremely interesting as it shows how extensively emigration from Bushwick and Williamsburgh had already swollen the population of neighboring Queens villages:

Maspeth .... 4,300  Newtown Heights ... 200  Corona Heights ... 500
Elmhurst ... 1,500  Corona ................ 2,928

The first years of the new century saw the final adjustments in routes and services that were to be made for many years to come. In November 1899 the B.R.T. drastically altered the transfer privileges and certain routings involving Maspeth depot. As of November 1st, all former transfer privileges at the depot were cancelled. The Flushing Ave. cars were terminated at the depot henceforth, no longer running through to Corona or Flushing village. The Grand St. cars were scheduled for through runs from the foot of Broadway to Corona. More important was the establishment of the later familiar Flushing-Ridgewood route out of the former Fresh Pond line routing cars through to Flushing instead of to North Beach as before. North Beach service then became a shuttle in winter and the eastern terminus of the Grand St. line in summer. Nor was this all. At Ridgewood depot passengers inbound on the Flushing-Ridgewood cars, Richmond Hill cars and Cypress Hills cars were permitted transfers to the Myrtle Ave. elevated only, and all former transfer privileges to other surface lines such as Bushwick, Myrtle and Gates Avenues were cancelled.

Sometime during 1900 the old Grand and Meeker line which had operated for 40 years through Humboldt and Meeker Avenues to Newtown Creek, was altered for half its length by the abandonment of the tracks in Humboldt St. Henceforth cars ran from Calvary Cemetery through Meeker Ave. and Nassau Ave.

Rebuilding of the bridge at Grand and Metropolitan Ave., January 1933. Car No. 3102 serves as a shelter for waiting passengers. Stanchions block the tracks.

The elevated railroad incline at Ridgewood, a view looking up the ramp from Cypress Ave. ,1906. *Robert Presbrey collection.*

to Manhattan Ave.; by 1907 this had been extended through Manhattan and Greenpoint Avenues to the ferry. The old Calvary Depot on Meeker Ave. went out of use at the same time after being in continuous service since 1861.

As the years passed, the Flushing Ave. cars, though normally terminated at Maspeth, extended their runs at certain hours and on special occasions. During the years when North Beach was the favorite resort on the north shore, Flushing Ave. cars ran through to the beach on Thursday evenings in summer for the fireworks displays, and also on sunny summer weekends. During the morning and evening rush hours some Flushing Ave. cars ran as far as Northern Blvd. up to as late as 1919.

There was very little change during 1900-1917 in car types; open cars, for example, were used on the Flushing Ave. line regularly each year, but never on the Grand St. or Flushing-Ridgewood lines. On Flushing Ave. the "2700" series cars were regularly used, a 10-window, double truck, semi-convertible type. For the long suburban runs on Grand St. to North Beach and on the Flushing-Ridgewood line, the "4100" series, built in 1906, was used, specifically 4101-4109 and 4122-4148, these being Brooklyn City cars. These trolleys were heavy, double-truck convertibles, and had high-powered headlights for country running.

Though service out as far as Corona was good, the Flushing people often complained of their end of the line. In July 1903 a resident declared that in the evening rush hour three eastbound Flushing Ave. cars came along to one of the Flushing-Ridgewood. When the Flushing-bound cars got to Ireland Mill Creek, the former inlet from Flushing Creek that once turned the grindstones of Ireland Mill, they would often be held up several moments by the crowds of boys using the trolley trestle as a diving board.

*A view looking north up Palmetto St. from a point below Seneca Ave., April 28, 1916. Charles Muller's saloon is on the right. Robert Presbrey collection.*

Coincident with the recent improvement in rolling stock was the expansion of facilities to house the cars. Late in 1906 the B.R.T. management came to the conclusion that the old wooden Maspeth Depot, built in 1885, was no longer equal to the increasing demands made on it. The building itself was a fire hazard and an expensive insurance risk; in spite of enlargement and some attempt at modernization during the 90's, the building offered little storage space and still less maintenance facilities. Contracts were let late in 1906 for an entirely new brick building on the corner of 69th St. (Brown Pl.) and Grand St. In February 1907 construction began and by December the new structure was finished. The completed building was two stories high with a facade of red brick; in shape it was triangular with a 50 ft. frontage on Grand St., 424 ft. on 69th St., 193 ft. along the rear, and 400 ft. on the east or storage yard side. Two tracks entered the building and expanded to eight inside, providing storage space for 45 cars. There was also an inspection pit passing under seven of the tracks, and a small machine shop in the rear equipped to handle everything except heavy overhauling and rebuilding. Because the normal complement of cars out of Maspeth Depot was 76 on the average and more in summer, a large open storage yard adjoining the new depot was added with a capacity of 105 cars. These were accommodated on 13 tracks served by six switches from a Grand St. lead track; through the center of this yard extended a fire wall for additional protection. With all these new facilities, Maspeth became even more important than before; at this time five lines operated out of the depot: Flushing-Ridgewood, Flushing Ave., Grand St., North Beach, and Metropolitan Ave.

Growth of population and the extension of rapid transit produced two new and beneficial changes on the Flushing-Ridegood line. In 1906 the B.R.T. extended the Myrtle Ave. elevated line from Wyckoff Ave. by utilizing the old private right-of-way of the former Bushwick R.R. along Palmetto St. The elevated was extended along Myrtle Ave. to just short of St. Nicholas Ave.; then curved over the old Bushwick R.R. car yard and then ran down a curved ramp into the Palmetto St private right-of-way, continuing at ground level to Metropolitan Ave. The new extension was opened on October 1, 1906.

The result of this elevated extension was to destroy the former Lutheran Cemetery trolley line running over the same route and to prevent the Flushing-Ridgewood cars from reaching Ridgewood Depot. After 1906 the Flushing-Ridgewood cars terminated at the private right-of-way at Fresh Pond Rd., and exchanged free transfers with the rapid transit line at the ground level station. This shortened the ride for patrons from Flushing, Corona and Elmhurst, and permitted travel from Park Row, Manhattan to Flushing Creek for 5 cents. For the next 9 years the trains continued to run at ground level. In May 1914, the B.R.T. began the elevation of this section between Wyckoff Ave. and Fresh Pond Rd. On February 22, 1915 the new elevated extension opened and the surface tracks remained in use only for shop movements.

Eloquent testimony to the growth of suburban Queens was the institution of all night service on the Flushing-Ridgewood line in June 1911. Previously the last car had left Fresh Pond Rd. for Flushing at 1:30 a.m., departing Flushing on it last trip at 2:00 a.m., going only as far as the Maspeth car barn. The new schedule provided for 15 minute headway until midnight, after which cars left Fresh Pond for Flushing at 12:30, 1:30 and 2:00 a.m., and then hourly until 5:00 a.m. Cars left Flushing for Fresh Pond at 2:30, 3:00, 4:30 and 5:00 a.m. This service required only one car, and it was nicknamed "Hawk".

At least part of the growth of population along the Flushing-Ridgewood line was stimulated by the extension of the I.R.T. elevated tracks along Roosvelt Ave. The 5 cent fare attracted settlement rapidly in the open areas of Elmhurst and Corona. The I.R.T. reached Queens Plaza on November 5, 1916 and 104th St Corona on March 21, 1917. The area along Junction Ave. and the Old Bowery Bay Rd. was slower to grow. In the summer there was heavy beach traffic, but the intervening land remained largely empty. So lonesome was the area that as late as 1911 a Wild-West style trolley hold up was successfully staged at 11:30 a.m. on April 28th at Astoria Blvd.

In the little community of Middle Village, the culminating event in the saga of trolley expansion in Queens took place. It was reserved for the Metropolitan Ave. line, almost the least noticed and certainly the most static in Queens, to give rise to the final extensive piece of trolley construction on Long Island. Since the 1880's Dry Harbor Rd. had been the terminal of the line. Beyond St. John's Cemetery the avenue was sparsely settled, yet as early as the 90's there were attempts made to induce the B.R.T. to consider extending to Jamaica.

The first serious efforts at extending the line eastward were made in 1907, when the B.Q.C & S. R.R. applied for a franchise. But it would be 9 years before the permits were granted and work begun.

In July 1916 the company announced that it would begin work and applied for permits. By mid-October, the work of erecting the trolley poles was progressing rapidly. By the end of November all poles had been installed, and work suspended until spring. In April 1917 track laying began and by the end of June the work was almost complete; one track was laid the full length the other half way. By mid-July both tracks reached Union Tpk.

On Tuesday, September 25, 1917 the new Metropolitan Ave. extension opened.

Bergen Street car No. 2755 signed "Georgia Ave." at the East New York car barns.

58

# MYRTLE AVE. & CYPRESS HILLS 1895-1917

Ridgewood at this time was a young community, scarcely ten years old and boomimg. The great railroad center at the corner of Myrtle and Wyckoff Avenues, which had been influential in the growth of the district during the 80's, continued to flourish and expand its services during the 90's. Population growth and street layout combined to make the "city line", as it was called, a remarkable terminal. By 1895 the Bushwick, Myrtle, Gates, and Union Ave. car lines all terminated here, in addition to the Myrtle Ave. elevated line. Besides these, there were three steam dummy routes, the Lutheran line, the Richmond Hill and the Cypress Hills line; then in June 1896 came the Flushing-Ridgewood line, and in January 1897 the Grand & Ridgewood line; when the latter was discontinued in 1899, the Flushing-Knickerbocker line took its place. In other words, no less than eight different surface lines and one elevated line all converged at this one point, making it a terminus with a traffic density and total number of cars, second only to Fulton Ferry or Williamsburgh Bridge Plaza.

In 1895 the Brooklyn City R.R. eliminated the last of the three steam dummy lines out of Ridgewood which had been running to the cemeteries since 1878 and 1881.

In May 1895 the company began erecting poles along Myrtle Ave, and service started on May 28th. Surprisingly, through service to Jamaica was given for a single 5 cent fare. This involved running Brooklyn City cars over Brooklyn, Queens Co. & Suburban tracks, an arrangement not often done in these early days.

In August 1895, the Lutheran line was converted to trolley operation. Electrification of this line made it possible a year later, in June 1896, for the Flushing-Ridgewood cars to come down the private right-of-way from Fresh Pond Rd.

When the Lutheran trolleys were put in service, a large gong was placed outside the Middle Village trolley station where the cars started for Evergreens(Ridgewood), and it was sounded each time an inbound car crossed the bridge over the L.I.R.R. tracks. This was to give notice to waiting passengers that a car was coming. The gong took the place of the old warning whistle on the dummies. Still more unusual was the installation of electric lights on the front of the waiting room in Middle Village in December 1895.

The Cypress Hills line was the last of the steam dummies to be eliminated. Conversion took place on October 27, 1895, marking the end of the era of steam dummy service on the B.R.T.

The short but interesting history of the parlor cars on the north side lines was paralleled on Myrtle Ave. during 1898. A group of businessmen, unhappy with the L.I.R.R. summer service, hit upon the idea of commuting to New York by private trolley. But even this glorious experience had to come to an end; on December 1, 1898 the "Amphion" made its last trip to Richmond Hill, and the charter service did not resume the following spring.

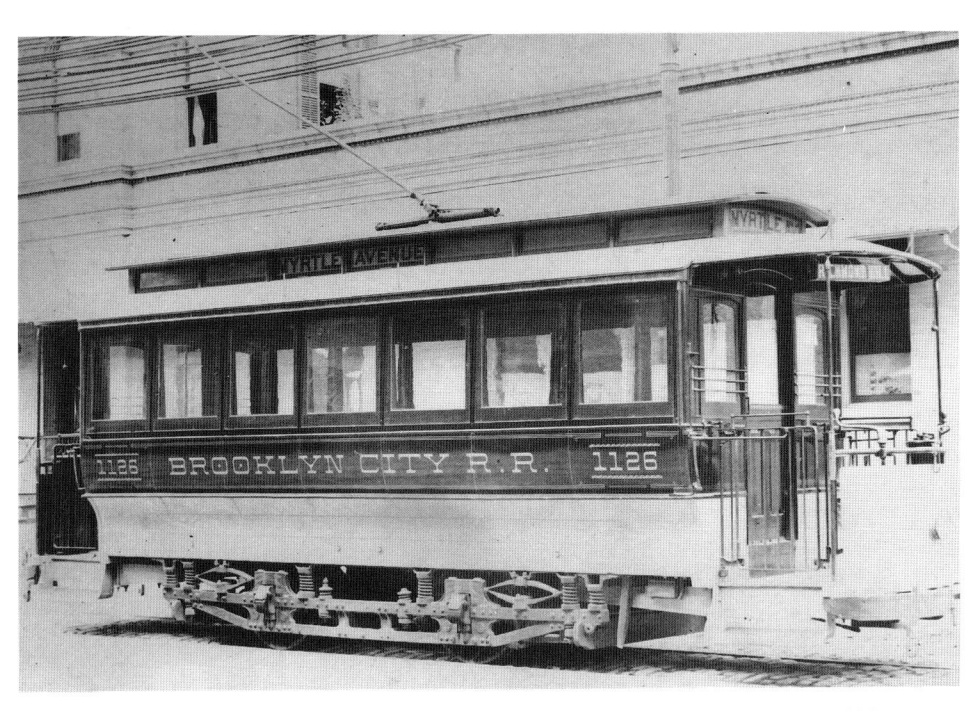

*B.C.R.R. No 1126 on the Myrtle Ave. line. Built by Lewis & Fowler in 1899. Edward Watson collection.*

Two disastrous fires in the Ridgewood area had a crippling effect on trolley operations. On Sunday December 27, 1896, fire broke out in the former Bushwick R.R. depot. When the B.R.T. had taken over the site in 1890, the horse stalls were removed and pits installed to lay up unused motor cars. The shed contained 10 tracks, on which were stored 16 open trailers, and four 20' closed motor cars. Thanks to the quick action of workers and firemen many of the motor cars, an electric sweeper and a snow plow were run out of the building and saved.

The second disaster occurred four years later in the Ridgewood power house. At 4:00 p.m. on Tuesday December 4, 1900, workers were startled when the lights all over the building blinked and then went out. Moments later, electricians discovered flames eating their way along the oil-soaked flooring. The fire spread so rapidly that the chief engineer barely had time to shut off the three big steam engines. The plant was totally destroyed, and as a result all power was cut off to Gates, Union, Myrtle, Flushing, Ridgewood, Putnam, Cypress Hills, Bushwick, Lutheran, Richmond Hill and Jamaica lines. From adjoining sheds scores of electric cars were pushed out by hand by B.R.T. workers and volunteer bystanders. Several hours later, emergency connections were made to the power lines of the Edison Co. and the Brooklyn City & Newtown R.R. to tide over the crisis.

In May 1901 all night service was instituted from Glendale to Richmond Hill. In February 1905 an express trolley service was initiated on Myrtle Ave. between Ridgewood Depot and Richmond Hill. To distinguish these cars from regular ones, a large iron sign reading "EXPRESS" was hung over the dash board. The express service ran at 10 minute intervals between 6:12 and 8:04 a.m. and 5:04 and 7:36 p.m. Only 8 stops were made: Ridgewood, Fresh Pond Rd.,, Cooper Ave., Golf Links, Glendale Park (88th St.), Woodhaven Ave., Terrace Park and Elm Ave. (114th St.)

One of the interesting features of trolley operation during these years was the growth and development of the transfer system. The original system was limited and had many weaknesses that were disadvantageous to the company. After some years of studying the situation, the B.R.T. on May 1, 1905 issued a new transfer ticket for the entire system. The new ticket was in two parts of different colors, part to be detached for use between 6 and 12 a.m., and the other part for afternoon use; the hours were stamped on and punched by the conductor. The new transfers were only half the size of the old ones, and became immediately popular with the ridership.

On June 1, 1914 the B.R.T. went further, by adapting the universal transfer system at the behest of the Public Service Commission (P.S.C.). In practice, this permitted transfers at Jamaica and Myrtle Avenues in either direction instead of one. Eastbound Jamaica Ave. passengers could transfer to westbound Myrtle Ave. cars without paying an additional fare.

It was in the early years of the century that the P.S.C. first comes into the picture with respect to trolley lines in Queens. The large size and power of the traction combines, generated a feeling of distrust and dislike by the public; as a result, a movement to regulate and oversee the companies snowballed into a legislative mandate. In 1906 the P.S.C. was set up, with one body to regulate New York City, and another the rest of New York State. In 1907 it descended on the trolley companies, probing every aspect of their organization and operations, and using its punitive power to force costly and extensive changes. Some of the improvements were long overdue; others were beyond the means of the companies and were contested in the courts. One of the earliest which predated the P.S.C. was the Thonet Bill,

signed into law in May 1905. It required the vestibuling of all street cars in Kings and Queens Counties; both front and rear platforms had to be enclosed and one-third of the work had to be completed by December 1905, or a penalty of $25 per car would be imposed.. Up to this time all car platforms had been entirely open; delightful in summer, but in winter and stormy weather the motorman had no protection. Since the law only required a screen or wind-shield between the dash and the roof, the companies did not contest the regulation. The B.R.T. began work in October 1905; one-third of the fleet was enclosed each year, and the task was completed by 1908.

In 1913 the P.S.C. sparked an improvement that was long overdue- air brakes. The traction industry had been producing heavier and heavier vehicles over the years, yet hand brakes were still being employed as the principal method to stop these increasingly larger cars. The installation of air brake systems was a complex, slow and expensive process, and the companies fought the order in court. The Supreme Court upheld the P.S.C. ruling in July 1913, and the companies were forced to install the requisite power brakes and geared hand brakes. The P.S.C. next ordered the installation of chemical fire extinguishers on all cars by September 15, 1913; again the companies appealed to the courts, and this time they won a stay.

The last significant regulation was the "near-side" ordinance of 1914. For years all street cars had crossed to the far side of the intersection and then picked up passengers through the rear doors; after September 1, 1914 cars stopped on the near side of the street and loaded through the rear.

The swifly passing years witnessed changes not only in the car equipment but in the cars themselves. The Richmond Hill line traffic was heavy enough from the very beginning to need larger double-truck cars; old single truck cars continued to service the Lutheran and Cypress Hills lines. In keeping with ladies fashion of the day, and at the insistance of the P.S.C. to lower car steps, the B.R.T. purchased 101 "hobble-skirt" or stepless cars in 1913 from Brill; the cars were numbered 3557, 5000-5099. These were the first center entrance cars on the Brooklyn system. In 1913, 50 of these cars were assigned to the Gates Ave. line, and were the first of their kind to be seen in Ridgewood. In September 1914 they were added to the Richmond Hill line to supplement the 4500 series convertibles which had supplied the basic service since 1907. In December 1915 the Richmond Hill line was the scene of an interesting experiment in articulated car use. Two old 1895 single truck Stephenson cars with 8 windows each, numbered 167 & 168, were rebuilt at the Fresh Pond shop into one articulated car and numbered 4900, after an earlier Boston model. A small compartment connected the front of one car to the rear of the other, and this

Car No.4800, affectionately known as *"Two-Rooms & ABath"*, was made from two single truck cars, No's 2358 & 2364, with a new center section added. While the idea worked very well for the Boston Elevated Railway, it was not a sucess in New York and the car was never duplicated and retired in 1925.

center compartment contained the entrance. This quaint car, after several trial trips, was put in regular service and dubbed "two-rooms-and-a-bath". The center compartment was connected to the end cars by two heavy leather diaphragms, which had openings at top and bottom that admitted the rain and wind. The two basic cars were too light, resulting in the poor riding quality of the combination. The passengers were given a jolting ride especially the standees, having to hang on to the straps, were flung about each time the articulation lurched.

Let us pause here, and take an imaginary trip along Myrtle Ave., beyond the city line. After leaving the car barns and storage yards on Wyckoff Ave, we come to Cypress Ave. and Kreuscher's Hotel, which survived into the 1920's as the Queens Labor Lyceum. Behind Kreuscher's Hotel on the south side of Myrtle Ave. is Ridgewood Park, which contained a dancing pavilion and bowling alley. A double track spur led into the park between Seneca and Cypress Avenues and ran to Weirfield St., where the tracks turned south to Wyckoff Ave. The park area was sold in 1911, and in 1912 was broken up into city blocks, ending an era.

Beyond Ridgewood Park was a great open area with virtually no buildings. We cross the L.I.R.R.'s Manhattan Beach Branch at grade an then proceed to Cypress Hills St. (old Fresh Pond Rd.) The new Fresh Pond Rd. was not cut through to Myrtle Ave. at the railroad until 1914-15. Ten blocks further brings us to the intersection of Cooper Ave., the beginning of Glendale, the site of considerable home building. Beyond Cooper Ave. there was nothing but farm land on either side of the road. Two-thirds of a mile further at the point where 88th St. and the present Interboro Parkway intersect was Glendale Schuetzen Park.

In our day of automobiles and extensive travel it is difficult to appreciate what these parks meant to the average worker in 1905, when private conveyances were beyond the means of all but the richest. Everyone worked six days a week, and Sunday was the great outing day, and for a little more than a dollar, a working man could take his family to some country grove in Queens and enjoy food , drink and song to his heart's content.

Emerging from the park we enter the beautiful suburban village of Richmond Hill. At the Jamaica Ave. terminus stands the Triangle Hotel, built in about 1874. This historic building still stands today, though not as a hotel.

As the years passed, and Ridgewood became more populated, the terminal facilities at Myrtle and Wyckoff Avenues became totally inadequate to handle the vast number of riders passing through this choke point twice daily during rush hours.

The first step taken by the company to better conditions was the extension of rapid transit to Metropolitan Ave. along the old Lutheran right-of-way. In 1905 the possibility was studied of bringing the Myrtle Ave. elevated to ground level above Wyckoff Ave. and continuing on to Metropolitan Ave.

In the summer of 1906 a curve was built over the car yards parallel to Woodbine St. and then into the private right-of-way, and the ramp from that point led the elevated tracks to ground level. From this point the elevated trains were to use the regular rails of the Lutheran line. On October 1, 1906 the new extension opened to the public. Wooden platform stations were built at Seneca Ave., Forest Ave. and Fresh Pond Rd.. In order to service the elevated cars at the end of the line, several acres of land were purchased adjoining the tracks between Fresh Pond Rd. and the L.I.R.R. A new storage yard and car shop was built, the beginning of the Fresh Pond Depot. Nine long storage tracks in the yard accommodated 100 cars, and the shop housed 36 more on its six tracks.

With the coming of the elevated, the old Lutheran line was superseded, and at the same time the Flushing-Ridgewood cars could no longer turn into the right-of-way and run to Ridgewood Depot. Flushing-Ridgewood cars now terminated at Fresh Pond Rd. at the elevated station, and free transfers were exchanged between the el and trolley. By the eve of World War I the population of the area was about 100,000 and Ridgewood Depot had become the largest and busiest on the system. It had 700 trainmen and 270 cars assigned to it. Sunday and holiday traffic ran as high as 50,000 passengers a day, due to the popularity of the picnic grounds and groves. The old depot buildings that were adequate when farms and country lanes predominated the area, now reached the saturation point.

Car No 3959 built by Stephenson Car Co. in 1905 for Nassau Electric R.R. *Vincent F. Seyfried collection.*

In 1914, to further cut down the crowding of the old Ridgewood Depot, another extensive improvement was undertaken. The first step was to elevate the whole Myrtle Ave. elevated operation, and secondly, to draw as many surface cars as possible to Fresh Pond Rd. and away from the Ridgewood barns. With the approach of World War I, automobile traffic began to be a factor, and wagon traffic remained as heavy as ever. Complaints about long lines of trolleys stored along Myrtle and Wyckoff Avenues appeared from time to time, because they blocked foot passage across the street, and were an eyesore to others. The great cavernous brick barns had become dingy and grimy with the passing years, and all car barn movements had to be made against busy street traffic. In August 1915 trouble broke out with the city over the B.R.T.'s occupation of Madison St. between Wyckoff Ave. and Irving Ave. Since the building of the car barns in 1881 Madison St. had been a lane between barn buildings, containing a spur track and interchange with the L.I.R.R. Since the street had never been legally opened, the B.R.T. had fenced it in. Over the years people had walked through to avoid a long detour. Early in August the B.R.T. put up a fence to keep intruders out, but property owners nearby appealed to the Highway Dept., which ripped the fence down. On August 6th the B.R.T. attempted to put up another, but were foiled by the police despite the company's protestations that they owned the fee to the road and that opening the street would isolate their storage yard.

Wearied with these difficulties and harassments, the B.R.T. resolved to pull out of the crowded old depot area as quickly as possible. On Sept. 2, 1913 the company began the elevation of the Lutheran section of the Myrtle Ave. elevated. The dangerous reverse curve across the car yards was removed and a single curve from Myrtle into Palmetto St. substituted. All the while that the elevated pillars and steel work were being installed, trains continued running along the ground without interruption. On Feb. 22, 1915 the new extension of the elevated line opened.

With the elimination of the Myrtle Ave. elevated trains from the ground, the surface tracks on the private right-of-way beneath were once again available for trolley use. The B.R.T. announced that, as soon as the Fresh Pond yards could be enlarged for the storage and servicing of trolleys, most of the car lines would be terminated at Fresh Pond Rd. rather than at Myrtle and Wyckoff. In the fall of 1914 the B.R.T. had acquired a large parcel of property adjoining the Fresh Pond yard. In January 1915 the new land at Fresh Pond was laid out to accommodate both surface and elevated cars. By the summer of 1915, eighteen tracks to store 700 cars were in place and in 1916 work on the trolley yard at the northwest corner was begun; this was to hold 200 cars.

The next bold move in the decentralization of facilities at Ridgewood was the building of a new trolley terminal in Glendale. In 1916 the B.R.T. bought the southwest corner of Myrtle Ave. and 72nd St. (Tesla Pl.) and built two spur tracks and a waiting room. The final step in the plan was the installation of a new trolley line along Fresh Pond Rd. between Myrtle Ave. and the private right-of-way, a stretch of six blocks. The section of Fresh Pond Rd. between Catalpa Ave. and Myrtle Ave. was itself very new, having been built in 1913-14 as a straightening of the old road.

Track laying proceeded very rapidly during the summer of 1916. On April 26, 1917 an extensive re-routing of most of the lines formerly terminating at Ridgewood was inaugurated. All Myrtle Ave. cars from downtown, plus the Wyckoff Ave. and Bushwick Ave. lines were routed through to the Tesla Place (72nd St.) terminal in Glendale. At the same time the Richmond Hill cars were diverted from Myrtle Ave. in Ridgewood to the new tracks in Fresh Pond Rd., all cars terminated under the Fresh Pond elevated station. Gates, Union, Cypress Hills, Flushing-Knickerbocker and Putnam Ave. lines continued to use the old Ridgewood Depot for the time being.

The B.R.T. now made its first move to abandon the Ridgewood Depot buildings. On the night of May 3, 1917 a track gang worked all night making track changes in front of the depot, and on May 4th the buildings were placed on the retired list.

Building the extension of the Myrtle Ave. El along the private right of way, on the block between St. Nicholas and Cypress ave. West side Nos 1863-1883 Palmetto. *Vincent F. Seyfried collection.*

Early in 1916 the company began laying new trolley track under the elevated extension and raised the former depressed roadbed at the same time without asking or notifying anyone. In May 1916 the matter came before the P.S.C. and the company was able to present a fait accompli. The city and the property owners immediately seized upon the company's "illegal" action to disclaim all responsibility for the cost, and the company quietly paid the bill as it had suspected would be the result all along.

Hardly had all these changes and improvements been made when the country became involved in the first World War. Within a very short time increases in passenger traffic and spiraling costs of materials placed new stresses and strains on the company, and within three short years almost transformed it completely.

Fresh Pond trolley yard as it looked just after opening in 1917, Middle Village is behind the yard in the distance. *Robert Presbrey collection.*

Diagram of the new B.R.T storage yard, November 1904. *Vincent F. Seyfried collection.*

# HARD TIMES AND RECEIVERSHIP
## 1918-1923

When the first World War broke out in Europe in 1914, most Americans viewed it as a far-off affair and congratulated themselves that America was traditionally free of European entanglements. For perhaps a year and a half the country played the role of disinterested spectator; then in 1916, as the conflict intensified, America began to feel the first economic effects. The Allied powers began to use America as an arsenal and war industries mushroomed overnight. As the demand for iron and steel, powder, chemicals, foodstuffs, textiles, etc., boomed, prices rose far above their 1914 levels. Closely linked to production was manpower. As the demand for skilled workers increased the wage rate rose proportionately.

The street railways were one of the first to feel the pinch. They were one of the largest consumers of iron and steel for tracks and rolling stock, and made heavy purchases of brass, copper, carbon, glass, etc., for line maintenance. Within three short years the price of street railway items skyrocketed astonishingly. The following are some examples:

| | | | |
|---|---|---|---|
| Axles | 101% | Feeder wire | 163% |
| Brakeshoes | 49% | Steel Poles | 215% |
| Car Wheels | 100% | Trolley Wire | 159% |

Not only did replacement parts become increasingly expensive, but difficulties arose at the same time on the labor front. Skilled car shopmen, experienced in machine and metal work and craftsmen of all sorts, began to drift away from the street railway car shops and take up new jobs in the expanding war plants where the wage rate was much higher. The trolley companies in order to hold their own men, had to raise their hourly rate to meet the competition. On Nov. 18, 1918 the B.R.T. raised salaries 20% to meet war plant wage scales and to offset the spiraling cost of living. Prices of every kind of farm product had gone up because of the immense Allied demand, and so had prices for necessities like shoes, clothing, durable goods and coal.

It was one thing to grant these increases but something else again to find the money. In 1917-18 the huge B.R.T. system employed about 11,800 men on its subway, elevated and trolley lines; with so large a work force even a small increase mounted to many millions. Nearly all the old franchises contained clauses stipulating a 5 cent fare, with no provisions for automatic increases because of changes in the economy. The B.R.T. had no remedy but to apply to the New York City authorities and the regulatory bodies for a modification of the franchise rate based on war hardship. In 1917 the first application was made to Mayor Hylan and the Board of Estimate for permission to raise the fare to 6 cents. In its appeal the B.R.T. pointed out the vast increase in the cost of service and the necessity to increase the number of runs on many of the lines because of war-stimulated travel. To show that this was not a local phenomenon, the company appended a list of other operating companies in other large American cities who had also applied for and received permission to charge 6 cents. The mayor took the application "under advisement" and did nothing. In May 1918 the B.R.T. again urged a 6 cent fare for its lines and submitted new statistics. No official decision was forthcoming; meanwhile the urgency increased. Two months later in July 1918 the B.R.T. filed another application with the Board of Estimate, this time for a 7 cent fare on all subways, els and surface lines. Meanwhile the company asked the Public Service Commission for permission to impose a 2 cent transfer charge. The great costs of raw materials needed for the maintenance of such an extensive system was again cited. On July 25th the B.R.T., issued a statement that in view of the four million dollar increase in operating expenses, service would be curtailed unless relief were granted; the cost of coal had risen one million dollars in 1918 and wages had risen three million. In answer to complaints that the service had degenerated, the company admitted it had too few crews to operate the cars because men had left for higher-paying jobs. Worse still, rails that had been ordered for urgently needed replacements had not been delivered by Bethlehem Steel Co. because of war priorities.

At this juncture the first wage increase was granted by the B.R.T. to stem the flight of crewmen to war plants. Conductors and motormen on the trolleys went from 30 cents to 40 cents an hour; subway and elevated men to 50 cents an hour effective August 2nd. The increase was granted largely in the anticipation of a fare rise that never came about.

Before the P.S.C. or the city could act on this new proposal, disaster struck, alienating all sympathy from the B.R.T. and its financial plight. Company policy up to this time had been more or less anti-union; no hostile action had been taken against any of the pioneer brotherhoods, but the officials distrusted the motives of professional organizers, who were not B.R.T. men, and whose interest lay solely in consolidating their own power and position. Early in October 1918 certain B.R.T. foremen had suspended 29 men for union activities on the job, and as a result a number of employees went out on a sympathy strike, hoping to tie up the system and force a reinstatement. About 20% of the motormen responded to the strike call and fewer trains had to be operated on longer headways. P.S.C. officials estimated that 90 men were out, but by adding more cars to the trains, service was kept to 80% of normal. At 2 a.m. on the morning of Nov. 2, 1918 the striking employees agreed to submit their entire case to the P.S.C. for settlement and return to work. At the same time the 29 men were ordered reinstated by the Federal War Labor Board.

As it happened, the B.R.T. found itself short of operating crews that Nov. 2nd, and a yard man came to be assigned as motorman on a Brighton Beach train during the evening rush hour. The five-car train left Brooklyn Bridge and made its first mistake at Franklin Ave. by continuing along the Fulton St. elevated, instead of turning into the Brighton tracks. This error corrected, all went well until the wooden cars approached the subway cut under Malbone St. (Empire Blvd.). For some reason the engineer dashed his train down the incline at such high speed that the forward cars left the rails and plowed into concrete abutments of the tunnel. Two of the wooden cars were sheared completely in half and the rest, badly damaged. Ninety-seven persons lost their lives and about 200 were injured.

The terrible toll of human life crowded even the war news off the front pages, and company and city officials hastened to the scene. Feeling ran high against the B.R.T. and all sorts of charges of recklessness, carelessness, etc., were leveled against the operating department. Several investigations were started, and when the fog of charges and counter-charges cleared away, the true facts emerged. Several high officials of the B.R.T. were indicted for manslaughter, but after long months of indictments were dismissed. The daily war communiques continued to monopolize public attention, and the disaster gradually faded from the pages, but the damage to the B.R.T.'s reputation had been done. It was fairly obvious that any hope of creating a favorable climate for a fare increase had been destroyed.

The Malbone Street wreck, the disaster that drove the BRT into bankrupcy. *Jeffrey Winslow* photo.

The Malbone St. wreck altered the financial position of the B.R.T. system immediately. A year of inaction on the part of the city administration had worsened the financial pinch, and the accident made certain a host of expensive damage suits and claims that would run into the millions. With no hope of a fare increase and with expenses mounting higher on every hand, there was but one thing to do: go into receivership. On Jan. 1, 1919 the huge Brooklyn Rapid Transit system succumbed to the inevitable and petitioned the courts for a receivership in bankruptcy. The War Finance Board set up by the Federal Government, had already advanced $17,320,500; when approached for an additional $10,000,000 the agency refused. The United States District Court in Manhattan under Judge Julius M. Mayer appointed Lindley M. Garrison, ex-Secretary of War in Wilson's cabinet from 1913 to 1916 as receiver. Garrison had been a lawyer all his life and had a distinguished career at the bar in both New Jersey and New York. The new receiver, on taking over, announced that the B.R.T. would continue to press for a 7 cent fare without which it could not meet its obligations.

During the first six months of 1919 Garrison worked hard to master the intricate organizational table and financial maze of the B.R.T. system. On July 14, 1919 the receivership was extended to the trolley lines, a move intended to preserve the unity of the system. The B.R.T. held $20 million in notes of the trolley underlying companies and foreclosing on these would have meant disruption of the system. The major underlying company, The Brooklyn City R.R., which, it will be remembered, was leased in 1893, was solvent, but placed under the control of the receiver never the less, to avoid breaking up the delicate complex of transfers, power facilities, etc.

On July 1, 1919 the Court of Appeals in New York handed down a decision that the Public Service Commission did have the power to raise rates in the matter of a 2 cent charge for transfers. With a clear-cut approval of the court of last resort behind it, the P.S.C. on July 19th gave the receiver permission to charge 2 cents for all but 30 of 1,008 transfer points beginning August 1st. Such permission was to last until July 30, 1920 and was estimated to bring in $1,600,000. Garrison announced that he would continue his fight for a 7 cent fare and engaged the engineering firm of Stone & Webster to survey the system.

On Aug. 1, 1919 at 5 a.m. the new system went into effect. All transfer points between elevated roads and the trolleys were kept undisturbed; 49 free transfer points were retained instead of 30; all free transfers were abolished between lines of subsidiary companies; between the same companies transfers were continued only when required by franchise or other considerations. Five Queens lines were ruled "feeder lines" and required to issue free transfers as follows:

Cypress Hills: to Bushwick, Flushing-Knickerbocker, Gates-Prospect park, Greene and Gates, Myrtle, Union, Wyckoff and Wyckoff Shuttle.

Richmond Hill: (at Myrtle and Fresh Pond) to Bushwick, Myrtle, Wyckoff (at Fresh Pond depot) to Flushing-Knickerbocker, Gates-Prospect Park, Greene and Gates, and Union Ave.

Grand St.: to Flushing Ave. or Flushing Ridgewood.
Metropolitan Ave.: on westbound trips to shuttle at Grand and Metropolitan.

Just as the new system was beginning to operate smoothly, trouble again hobbled the B.R.T.; many employees, dissatisfied with the wage rise of August 1918, began to consider joining a strong union and pressing for additional increases. A unit of the American Association of Street & Electrical Railway Employees was organized and its leader soon claimed 60% of the working force. Big wage rises had been secured in Boston, Detroit, Cleveland and Chicago and the news brought dissatisfaction to Brooklyn men. They, of course, overlooked the fact that in all these cities there had been fare increases.

On the evening of Aug. 1, 1919 about 1,000 men met and voted to send a committee to Garrison, threatening a strike unless the B.R.T. agreed to union recognition, a 75 cents hourly wage scale and an 8 hour day. There was a great deal of whistling, stamping, and clapping, and it was voted to give Garrison until Tuesday the 5th to reply. Many men thought the slender increase in revenue from the 2 cent transfer charges would finance a wage rise for everybody. It happened that Garrison was out of the city and the operating officials began preparing for a strike and sought police protection.

On the August 5th deadline Garrison informed the union that he would meet none of their demands; since the property was in the custody of the Federal Courts, he asked for 500 deputy marshalls to supplement the police. The employees declared the strike would continue until the B.R.T. agreed to recognize the union and negotiate with it. The power house men were 60% organized and ready to strike. All police leaves were canceled by the city. Towards dawn of the 6th the union sent out flying squads to tour the depots and stop all service.

At first the strike seemed a failure, as service seemed almost normal during rush hour. Then quick raids by strikers at different depots frightened crews till they refused to take cars out. Dashing about in motor trucks, the strikers cut trolley wire, bell ropes, dragged conductors and motormen from the cars and blocked the tracks with piles of asphalt. When faced with a total shutdown, the order was given to place policemen on each car or train. By this time control of the situation had been lost. The strikers were aggressive and moved swiftly in motorcycles. Thousands of riders waited in the rain for trains that failed to come; at 10 p.m. all service was halted.

Trolley service in Brooklyn was poor except on the lines operating out of Crosstown depot, which still had normal service on the Graham, Greenpoint, Crosstown, Calvary Cemetery, Meeker and Nassau Avenue lines. In Queens Fresh Pond depot was the hardest hit with 23 out of 99 runs knocked out. Service on the Metropolitan Ave. line was almost entirely suspended. Almost normal service prevailed on the Grand St. and Flushing-Ridgewood lines, then towards evening the later line was almost entirely suspended. On the system as a whole, 640 out of 892 cars were running and of these 374 had police aboard.

On August 7th the tie-up was complete. Only 236 of 1,286 trolleys operated and nearly all elevated and subway lines were out. By the next day, little had changed, still fewer trolleys ran. On the 9th Garrison was prevailed upon to meet with the strikers. By this time only 41 cars were running, only 2 were out of Fresh Pond.

That night it was announced that Garrison had yielded and the strike was settled. The union was assured of recognition by the B.R.T., and the chief stumbling block was removed. A 25% wage increase was given with the approval of the commission and the court.

With the strike over, the badly-shaken B.R.T. settled down to only brief peace. Financially, the company was in such poor condition that collapse was but a matter of weeks. On Oct. 1, 1919 the quarterly rental of $300,000 due to the bondholders of the Brooklyn City R.R. trolley lines fell due, and the B.R.T. was unable to make payment. Receiver Garrison notified Federal Judge Mayer of the situation and Mayer ruled that the vast B.R.T., intact since 1896, would have to be broken up in view of the fact that it could not meet its obligations. Mayor Hylan as usual fulminated about "traction rings" but an investigation revealed that the "ring" owning the Brooklyn City property consisted of 1,572 holders, 742 of them women who were widows living on the income, and 197 estates.

The legal and financial and even physical separation of the Brooklyn City R.R. properties from the rest of the system was an extremely complex and difficult task. In the 30-odd years that had elapsed since the lease of 1893, the properties had become so intertwined and intermingled that no one really knew just where a line of demarcation could be drawn. Many lines had been merged, extended and blended with one another in the process of transit growth and modernization and the prospect of disentangling all this loomed as not only complex but highly undesirable from the point of view of good service.

The Brooklyn City R.R. accounted for 35 trolley lines and shuttles in all, scattered through Brooklyn and Queens Counties. There was some speculation at first that the Brooklyn, Queens Co. & Suburban would also be involved with its nine surface lines, for, under the terms of the agreement of 1893 between the Brooklyn Heights and the Brooklyn City, when the holding company (Brooklyn Heights) had secured permission to use some of the Brooklyn City guarantee fund to acquire the B.Q.C. & S., it agreed in payment to turn over to the Brooklyn City at the expiration of the leases of its lines, all stock of the Suburban Company owned by it (Brooklyn Heights). In other words, the Brooklyn City was entitled to full ownership of the B.Q.C. & S. because its money had been used by the Brooklyn Heights to buy out the Suburban properties. There was some speculation too that the B.R.T. would default on its Nassau Electric R.R. obligations as well.

On Oct. 1, 1919 at Judge Mayer's order, the 35 Brooklyn City R.R. lines became a separate and distinct organization with their own general manager. The changes produced by this separation were the most far-reaching and drastic known in Brooklyn since the 90's. Nearly all of the free transfer points were abolished, and since the B.R.T. and the Brooklyn City were separate and distinct properties, no transfers between them were permissible. About 600 transfer points were abolished in all; the B.R.T. continued to charge the 2 cent transfer rate between its own lines. For many patrons the fare rose to 10 cents unless such persons could manage to travel the whole distance back and forth to work on cars of one company. Two long lines in Queens were broken into two zones:

| | | |
|---|---|---|
| Grand St.: | Zone I Broadway Ferry to Newtown Creek | 5 cents |
| | Zone II Newtown Creek to North Beach | 5 cents |
| Flushing Ave.: | Zone I Park Row to Onderdonk Ave. | 5 cents |
| | Zone II Onderdonk Ave. to Maspeth | 5 cents |

In one case the fare was lowered: the Flushing-Ridgewood zone line at Flushing Creek was abolished, and 5 cents charged for a through ride from Flushing through to Ridgewood. The former trolley terminals at Fresh Pond depot and Cooper Ave., Glendale, (Tesla Pl.) were abolished to avoid the collection of a second fare on those Brooklyn lines which had to go a short distance into Queens to terminate there. The following were the lines affected and their new terminals:

Bushwick Ave.: cut back from Tesla Pl. to Myrtle & Wyckoff Ave.
Flushing-Knickerbocker: discontinued altogether.
Flushing-Ridgewood: extended down Palmetto St. to Wyckoff Ave.
Richmond Hill: extended along Myrtle Ave. to Wyckoff Ave.
Union Ave.: terminated at Myrtle and Wyckoff Avenues. Cut back from Fresh Pond Rd.

Wyckoff Ave.: cut back from Tesla Pl. to Myrtle and Wyckoff Avenues.
Wyckoff Shuttle: discontinued altogether.
Greene & Gates: cut back from Fresh Pond Rd. to Myrtle and Wyckoff Avenues.
Myrtle Ave.: cut back from Tesla Pl. to Myrtle and Wyckoff Avenues.

The following three points were allowed to stand in Queens County:

1. At Flushing Ave. and Grand St. between Flushing and Grand cars but only to passengers paying cash fares east of Newtown Creek.
2. Flushing Ave. and Fresh Pond Rd. between the Flushing and Flushing-Ridgewood cars but only to passengers paying cash fares east of Onderdonk Ave.
3. At Junction and Corona Avenues, Corona, between Grand St. and Flushing-Ridgewood cars.

So extensive were these changes in Brooklyn that two weeks were spent on the details of planning and organizing before attempting to implement them. Although the Brooklyn City R.R. was entitled under the terms of the old franchise, to charge a separate fare at each former village boundary line, it wisely avoided excessive charges on any one line; 10 cents was the maximum on the longest. On October 16th transfers between the surface roads and elevated lines were stopped. In Queens this meant that trolley patrons transferring at Fresh Pond depot to the Myrtle Ave. el had to pay a second fare.

On October 18, 1919 Judge Mayer signed the formal order of separation, effective at midnight the same day. On the first morning of the new order, all went smoothly thanks to extensive publicity in the local newspapers of Brooklyn and Queens.

With the departure of the Brooklyn City R.R. and its physical properties an accomplished fact, The B.R.T. bent its efforts to managing the subway, elevated and remaining trolley lines. A study was commissioned, and the firm of Stone & Webster was retained to investigate the condition of the company. It reported that nothing less than an 8 cent fare could restore the lines to financial stability. Continuation of the 5 cent fare on the trolley lines would create a deficit of $5,326,000 annually by June 30, 1922. In view of the 25% increase in wages, plus taxes, expenses and fixed charges, only an 8 cent fare coud keep the system solvent. Federal judge Mayer made the report public and announced his intention to keep fighting for a fare that would insure survival of the properties. He pointed out that the B.R.T. was obligated, under contracts with the city, to construct extensions and build new lines, but with the present 5 cent fare,

no interest was being paid on the bonds and no money set aside for rapid transit imporovement. The surface lines were estimated to earn only 40% of their fixed charges.

Shortly thereafter the B.R.T. found itself with another strike on its hands. In the contract of August 1919 with the union, the company granted the workers the right of arbitration on matters of wages and hours. This right Judge Mayer and Receiver Garrison had refused to recognize except under certain conditions which they held to be legally necessary, in view of the fact that the B.R.T. was in receivership. They insisted that the wage issue could not be decided soley by arbitration due to the financial state of the company.

The workers felt that they were due a pay increase, as their last was in August 1919, and decided to go on strike against the advice of union leaders. The strikers struck so quickly that in a short time surface lines were completely shut down and only 61 two-car trains operated.

On September 1st, the second day of the strike, management offered to arbitrate all but wage demands. The union suggested a 10% wage increase and direct negotiations, but Judge Mayer refused to deal with the strikers or their leaders. The next day Garrison announced that he would do no bargaining unless the men returned to work, and made determined and successful efforts to restore service. As many as 75 cars operated on 7 lines, and rapid transit service improved to 15% of normal.

On the 3rd Judge Mayer made an offer of an 8% wage increase and collective bargaining of all issues, but the strikers remained defiant and spurned the offer. By this time 20 surface lines had been opened, and a trickle of men began to return to work. In Queens, only the Richmond Hill line was operating.

As the days passed, the strike settled down to a deadlock. The B.R.T. hired about 3,000 strikebreakers to man the cars, and as result service picked up daily. On September 7th Bushwick Ave. opened with 13 cars, Flushing-Ridgewood and Grand Ave. with 10 each. The line continued to refuse to deal with the strikers directly and advised them that September 8th was the last day the men could return to work without loss of seniorty; more than 1,000 returned to work.

By September 9th, the tenth day of the strike, 51 trolley lines were running with 737 cars; and service was about 75% of normal on trolley lines and 88% on rapid transit.

On September 13th the B.R.T. management struck back hard. A big advertising campaign was launched to recruit a large force of new men for permanent employment, and training facilities were greatly expanded. Meanwhile, service began at night. The union had made boasts that a million dollar reserve was available for strike benefits, but when it came time to distribute the money, only $10,000 could be scraped up and large numbers of the strikers returned to their jobs when offered $3 a week in strike benefits. by the 18th, 4,141 men had returned to work and 1,005 new ones hired, with 3,500 strikebreakers still on the payrolls. By the third week of the strike service was nearly normal, and the strike was all but over. The strike leaders promised all sorts of inducements to keep the strike going, but at this point no one believed them. On the 24th the Flushing-Ridgewood, Grand and Flushing lines had all night service restored; and Richmond Hill and Myrtle Ave. on the 26th.

At the end of the month the strike was dead in fact and it was possible to assess the results. Seven thousand men had returned to work and all the strikebreakers had been discharged; about 2,200 new men had been hired. The union had been so discredited and beaten that it lost all its members in the B.R.T. organization. Although the company had destroyed all organized opposition and forced a return to work on its terms without a wage increase, the effort cost dearly. The strikebreakers manning the cars that operated during the first two weeks kept all the fares for themselves, some making as much as $25 a day. The company was in no position to force collections, as the strikebreaking agency was in nominal charge of its own men. A typical crew might turn in from 10 to 25 cents as a gesture, and the company really didn't expect to receive anything more. Crews complained that few routes really paid and that the conductor had to split with the motorman, the policeman on the car, the starter, and the men in the barns

In Queens the strike hit hard because the trolleys were the backbone of local transit and no substitute existed. Workers had to hitch rides as best they could, on trucks and private autos; many truck owners made improvised buses of them and charged from 25 to 75 cents per ride.

Although the Flushing-Ridgewood and Grand St. cars had resumed running on September 7th, management seemed content on letting the North Beach (Junction Ave.) segment lie unoperated. After much local complaining the line was quietly reopened on October 8, 1920.

The five-week long strike of September 1920 made the B.R.T.'s finances even more precarious than before, and as an economy measure, Receiver Garrison decided not to resume service on nine of the former strike-bound lines on the ground that they did not pay and that running them would be a drag on the others that barely paid their way. The P.S.C. started hearings under pressure from local civic associations but Judge Mayer gave legal approval to Garrison's move. These lines included the Church, Ocean, Metropolitan, 39th St. Ferry-C.I., Wyckoff, Park, Hicks, 7th Ave. and the two shuttle - Broadway Ferry and Ralph Ave. As a result of the P.S.C. hearings Commissioner Nixon ordered service resumed, but Judge Mayer stepped in with an injunction forbidding the P.S.C. to issue a resumption order without an action in Mayer's Federal Court.

So far as Queens was concerned, Metropolitan Ave. alone was affected. As a compromise Receiver Garrison agreed to reopen that part of the line between Flushing Ave. and Dry Harbor Rd. (80th St.), which was done on Oct. 28, 1920. The Middle Village residents had brought heavy pressure on the P.S.C. and the commission had finally issued an order as of October 20th directing the B.R.T. to resume service. The restored line was little more than a shuttle service of 2 1/2 miles but was better than nothing. Continued complaints in Brooklyn of the stoppage of trolley service, especially on Church and Ocean Avenues, sparked a legislative investigation by the State Legislature. Receiver Garrison welcomed the members and gave them all sorts of materials to study. It was learned that $4,296,066 of reserve funds had been used to operate the road during the strike, and that it would take at least $4 million to rehabilitate the properties. In February 1921 Garrison proposed limiting the 5 cent fare to Old Brooklyn, suggesting that additional nickels be collected at the old town lines. Garrison offered to reopen Metropolitan Ave. if it were made a two-fare line. After long hesitation and many hearings the P.S.C. finally authorized two fares on Metropolitan Ave., and the receiver then opened the line to Jamaica Ave. on March 18, 1921; the Myrtle Ave. elevated terminal at Lutheran Cemetery was made the zone point. Finally, on April 6, 1922 the remainder of Metropolitan Ave. was opened between Flushing Ave. and Williamsburgh Bridge.

To effect further economies, Receiver Garrison announced the necessity of cutting wages in July 1921. If the 5 cent fare were to be retained as the city and the Transit Commission required, a wage cut of 10% was immediately necessary; this plus a fall in the post-war market of raw materials would place the system on a sound financial basis. The company and the union consulted together on the reduction and the 11,000 members accepted a cut provided it did not exceed 10%. As of Aug. 5, 1921 the new rates for older men were 45 cents to 67 cents; for new men 45 cents to 55 cents. The B.R.T. estimated a saving of $2,500,000 in wage costs.

The year 1922 showed such a heartening increase in net income on both the surface and rapid transit lines that the Federal Court began to make plans to end the receivership.

The B.R.T. in the last six months of 1921 had an increase of 1/4 million over 1920, but to produce this gain, from 50 to 60 fewer cars were run and more passengers had to stand.

On Feb. 9, 1923 Judge Mayer took the first step toward ending the receivership by announcing the completion of a reorganization plan prepared by the Stockholders' Committee. The plan envisaged appropriations to operate the company, fund all obligations, pay interest, claims, etc., and pay off receiver's certificates. Provision was made to include the Brooklyn City surface lines at a later date. The plan was the outcome of months of negotiations and most interested groups had signified approval.

On May 24, 1923 the Brooklyn-Manhattan Transit Co. was incorporated at Albany as the reorganization corporation to take over and operate the old B.R.T. It was also agreed to scale down the bonds and notes outstanding to reduce the fixed charges, exchange old stock for new, and pay off $2 million in Malbone St. claims. On June 5th the Transit Committee announced its satisfaction with the reorganization and approved the B.M.T. Co.

To the pleasure and satisfaction of all interested parties, the receivership was ended on June 14, 1923. Garrison was warmly thanked for a difficult job well done and much praise went to Federal Judge Mayer for a careful and wise administration of a complex property. Editorials praised the harmony of the entire four and a half year receivership and the present healthy condition of the road despite war, strikes and troubles. Traffic had increased 50%. Reviewing the betterments to the system, Mayer commented that approximately $1,600,000 had been spent on the surface lines for track reconstruction, new cars and rebuilding.

The Brooklyn City R.R., meanwhile, now that it had been determined that it was in the best interests of the stockholders to remain independent of the reorganized B.M.T., announced a wage increase effective August 3rd of four to five per cent for about 2,500 motormen and conductors. The new rates ranged from 50 cents to 62 cents per hour. In addition, $5 million was earmarked for special track work, new cars and conversion of old cars.

On Dec. 22, 1923 the Brooklyn, Queens County & Suburban R.R. was also taken out of receivership and placed in the control of the new B.M.T. With this move all the Queens surface lines of the old B.R.T. were free of legal and financial trouble and a new post-war era opened that was to bring to the trolley lines a greater prosperity than they had ever known before.

# THE LAST YEARS - 1923-1948

With the turbulent period of receivership and labor unrest safely behind, the new B.M.T. Co. entered upon an era of serenity in management and comparative stability in routing. The drastic changes of 1919-1921 became permanent and accepted and there remains for us to chronicle little more than routine practices and temporary adjustments.

To the spectator, the most remarkable change on the B.M.T. system during the period between the two wars was the extensive modernization in the trolleys themselves. The emphasis in all post-war traction operation all over the United States was economy, speed and safety. The older vehicles were very heavy, drew a great deal of power, started slowly, and lent themselves to many boarding and alighting accidents.

An engineer for the management firm of Stone & Webster, one Charles O. Birney, achieved temporary fame in 1916-17 with his designs for a cheap, light-weight, one-man safety car. The new Birney car, as it came to be called, achieved instant popularity all over the county. Not only did it draw little power, but it eliminated the services of a conductor, thus halving labor costs.

During the receivership, Garrison heard of the Birney cars and their fine performance record, and ordered six cars as an experiment. The first four were placed in service on the 65th St.-

Birney car #7155. These small-capacity cars were used on the Cypress Hills and Flushing-Ridgewood lines in the 1920's. Photographer unknown.

*Birney car No 7151 at the end of the Cypress Hills line, July 31, 1935, the last day of service under that name. Vincent F. Seyfried collection.*

Ft. Hamilton line on February 24, 1919; for the time being, it was decided to use the cars on light lines in the outlying districts. The new cars were liberally patronized and it was remarked that they stopped and started more easily than the older cars. The Brooklyn City R.R. observed the new cars progress over six months, and decided to order an additional 108 cars. The B.R.T. also ordered 92 at the same time. Improvements were ongoing, and the low cost of the cars combined with their enviable safty record made them irresistible. By the middle of December operation of the new cars had begun on Brooklyn City lines. By January 1920, the B.R.T. had already placed 200 of the cars in service at a cost of $1,245,000. 108 cars were allocated to the Brooklyn City (7000-7107); 73 to the Nassau Electric lines (7108-7180); 11 to the Coney Island & Brooklyn (7181-7191); and the remainder to the Brooklyn, Queens County & Suburban (7192-7199).

The great savings in platform costs resulting from elimination of the conductor persuaded the Brooklyn management to convert as many of its old serviceable cars as possible to one-man operation. The open platform and gates were removed, and folding doors installed; it also meant the conversion of the cars to front entrance rather than the old rear entrance procedure. Cars could not be converted to one-man operation unless they were fitted with the safety devices and safeguards found on the Birney cars. By June 15, 1923, 150 older cars had been converted.

*B&QT No 2541 in the car yard. A. Gilcher photo.*

In 1923 the Brooklyn City embarked on an ambitious program of new car procurement; 200 new cars were ordered from Brill and St. Louis Car Companies, based on the designs of a transit engineer from Baltimore, Peter Witt. The new cars were a double truck, center entrance, drop center, arch roof design. The first cars were delivered in January 1924. By that time the Brooklyn City lines were carrying 21 million riders annually.

*B&QT No 2708 in the car yard. A. Gilcher photo.*

71

The new cars were numbered in the 8 thousand series, 8000-8099 were built by Brill and 8100-8199 by St. Louis Car Co. So successful were these cars in hauling large crowds through heavy traffic that an additional order was placed in 1925 for 150 additional cars from Brill (8200-8448) and 85 additional from Osgood-Bradley. This extensive modernization of the trolley fleet allowed the B.C.R.R. and the B.M.T. to retire hundreds of older obsolete cars. Many of these old cars were burned or dumped into swamps; in April 1924 employees were offered as many old trolley bodies as they liked for $25 each, for conversion to summer cottages.

The 8000 series Peter Witt cars eventually replaced the older cars on almost every line of the far-flung B.M.T system, even replacing the newer Birney cars. Time and experience had shown that the Birneys had a distressing tendency to gallop at speed, as a result by 1937 all Birneys had been replaced by Peter Witts.

In Queens the older cars lingered on; the 2500 series ran on Junction Ave. until World War II, and on Jamaica Ave. till 1940. The Cypress Hills line was never worth modernizing, and 2700 series cars ran to the end in 1947. Metropolitan, Flushing-Ridgewood, Grand and Richmond Hill lines received 8000 series cars in the early 30's and ran them to the end.

Car No 8400 on Myrtle Ave. near Fresh Pond Rd., October 3, 1948. *Vincent F. Seyfried collection.*

*Above:* PCC #1016 at Coney Island. These operated from Brooklyn lines into Queens only in special service to the 1939 World's Fair. *Right:* B&QT trolley terminal for the 1938-1939 World Fair, at Lawrence St., now College Point Blvd. *R. Presbrey* photo.

The Presidents' Conference Car or PCC was the final development in street railway vehicle design. It was the Brooklyn system that pioneered the introduction of these ultra-modern cars. By 1929 it was obvious that the street railway industry was dying; great numbers of small lines all over the country had perished; the hope of the future lay only in larger cities where the tremendous traffic densities favored retention of street cars. In 1929 a group of electric railway presidents gathered and agreed to finance research into designing a totally modern trolley completely free of noise and the defects of traditional cars.

After five years of work and one million dollars, the PCC car emerged. Its chief features were a streamlined appearance, almost completely silent, smooth acceleration, powerful brakes and many automobile like features in trim and appearance. On October 1, 1936 the first twenty PCC cars entered service on the Smith-Coney Island line in Brooklyn. Not long after 100 cars were in service on four Brooklyn lines. The PCC never saw regular service in Queens, they came to Queens only on one occasion: May 1, 1938, on the official opening of the World's Fair grounds, to help publicize the new and expanded service to the fair.

On two occasions during the early 20's the entire surface system in Queens ground to a halt because of power failure. A blow-out occurred at the B.M.T. power house at 5 p.m. on July, 23, 1922 stalling cars along Grand St., Flushing Ave., and parts of the Flushing-Ridgewood line. The tie up lasted only an hour, before emergency repairs restored service.

The last known breakdown occurred two years later on Sunday afternoon, June 22, 1924, when a small fire in the switch room of the Kent Ave. power station got out of control and took firemen two hours to combat. The Fulton, Lexington and Myrtle Ave. elevateds and all trolley lines in north Brooklyn and Queens were out of service for three hours.

The last system wide event of importance occurred in 1929. On May 11 application was made to the Transit Commission by the Brooklyn City R.R., the Nassau Electric R.R., the Coney Island & Brooklyn R.R., the Brooklyn, Queens County & Suburban R.R. and the Coney Island & Gravesend R.R. for approval of a merger and consoladation of their capital stock, franchises and propery under the name and ownership of a new corporation to be known as the Brooklyn & Queens Transit Co. (B.&Q.T.). The commission approved and the merger becamer effective July 1, 1929. This brought to an end the corporate existance of the old independent companies which had merged into the old B.R.T. from the 90's on and existed in name only during the last 30 years.

73

# A Review Of The Final Decades Of Trolley Operation In Queens 1920-1947

## FLUSHING-RIDGEWOOD

One of the largest rehabilitation projects of the 1920's was the realignment of Fresh Pond Rd. When trolleys first began on it in 1896, the road was a country lane twisting and turning, bordered by an occasional farmhouse. Over the years contractors building houses and stores along the road had straightened it somewhat. As a result, the trolley tracks which had been laid in 1893 followed the contours of the original road. They rambled all over the width of the road and in some places were on the sidewalk.

Birney No 7106, looking north into 61st. St. from Mt. Olivet Ave. May 1922. *Robert Presbrey collection.*

Another change occurred in 1928 when the National Ave. spur was removed. This little one block, double track segment ran from Corona Ave. north to the Corona L.I.R.R. station, and had been the original terminus in 1896. At the same time the sharp near right angle turn along the south line of Corona Ave. was eliminated.

The growth of Queens as a residential area occasioned numerous street openings in the 1920's in order to install sewers. Besides the break of 1918, a further project in 51st Ave., Elmhurst, made service difficult. In October 1921 service was maintained over a single track in the vicinity of Broadway and 51st Ave. and two temporary crossovers were installed at the library building and some hundred feet east of Broadway in Corona Ave.

The year 1919 saw the Flushing-Ridgewood line the victim of the last known trolley holdup in Wild West style. At 4:15 a.m. on February 4th five masked and heavily armed desperadoes boarded a car at Flushing terminus and robbed the conductor, motorman, and several passengers. Several hours previously at 10:45 p.m. the same band help up and robbed the crew and passengers of a North Beach car. One thug boarded the back platform and one the front, while the three others lined up the passengers at gun point. The robbery had a peculiarly modern touch - the get-away was made in a green automobile. About a week later careful detective work led the police to a Brownsville hideout where the men, all 17 to 24 years old, were arrested.

At the court hearing the judge, determined to make Queens trolley riding safe, sentenced the leader to 40 years, another 28, a third 26, and the others 10-19 years each. The two robberies had netted only $150, and after dividing the loot, each youth got only $11.20 each!

In June 1921 the operator of a Birney car crossing the lonely meadows saw six men in a big touring car signal him to stop. Instantly suspicious, he raced to the other end of the car, grabbed his switch iron and attacked the party as they prepared to board. He then reversed the car and raced to Corona and a police station. When the car returned to the scene, the six men and their touring car had fled.

The Flushing-Ridgewood and the North Beach line were among the first to be assigned Birney cars in 1919. The local residents were not by any means pleased at the change; an editoral remarked that "they are providing wholly inadequate to the traffic on that division, and as a result, there are loud protests over the bad service, particularly during the morning and evening rush hours." The B.R.T. ignored these protests and in September 1921 a renewed complaint was made by the Ridgewood Heights Improvement Association regarding the crowded condition of the Birneys, the unsanitary crowding, and danger in overloading a car designed to seat only 32. In spite of these recurrent protests the Birney car seems to have stayed on until the late 20's when it was replaced with the larger 8000 series cars.

The year 1925 saw the appearance of the first real bus competition in Elmhurst, Corona and Jackson Heights. For 30 years and more the Brooklyn City R.R. and the L.I.R.R. had shared between them a near monopoly of travel, but on July 9, 1925 the Fifth Avenue Bus Corp. of Manhattan opened its first Queens line between Jackson Heights and Manhattan on a 10 cent fare. As the empty lots began filling up rapidly with the extension of transportation, the Fifth Avenue Co. opened up additional routes north and south of Corona Ave.

Despite the competition the Flushing-Ridgewood line gained steadily in traffic during the 20's and 30's thanks to intensive home building all along the line. From a post-war low of 5,301,989 in 1921, passengers reached a peak of 10,059,427 in 1931, a 100% increase in only ten years.

Thanks to the opening of the World's Fair 1939-40, the Flushing-Ridgewood line rose to major importance suddenly. The site chosen for the Fair was the extensive series of meadows all along Flushing Creek from the bay south to Queens Blvd., a vast meadow land which had been in the process of filling in since 1915. A vast tract to be graded, paths laid out, foundations sunk, etc., and in the process, the alignment of the old Strong's Causeway came to be drastically altered. In 1924 a new highway had been laid out, going in a straight line from Queens Blvd. at 61st Ave. to the causeway bridge; when opened, the new road received the name Nassau Blvd. The old bridge, however, was left intact and so was the old Strong's Causeway along 63rd Rd., Apex Pl. and 62nd Dr.

*Flushing-Ridgewood car #8317 climbing out of College Point Blvd. onto the L.I.Expressway during the 1939 World's Fair. Sidney Silleck photo.*

In 1938 the old Nassau Rd. was widened to four lanes for its whole length and the old road and bridge across the meadows was destroyed. A new road was laid out at about the same crossing point but six lanes wide, and it was carried for part of the way across the meadows on a steel bridge so as not to bisect the Fair Grounds. The new highway received the name Horace Harding Blvd. and the trolley tracks were realigned to occupy a position on either side of the sidewalks. Two new turnouts were built, one on either side of the highway, just under the foot-bridge that conducted passengers from the elevated line on Roosevelt Ave. to the Fair Grounds. These sidings enabled loaded cars to discharge passengers without obstructing other cars. A second and larger siding with additional spur tracks and a loop was built on Rodman St., Flushing, at 58th Ave. to handle Fair traffic and the many extra cars; a dispatcher's office and rest room were also erected at the site. On May 1, 1938 these new facilities were officially opened with a procession of trolleys led by PCC cars #1044 and #1079.

By the end of 1938 the new roads, access paths, realignments, etc., had been completed and the Fair Grounds opened on schedule in 1939. The trolleys carried the heaviest traffic in years to and from the Fair, and for the summer months of 1939-40 the Flushing-Ridgewood line was easily the best revenue earner in Queens. The shadow of war hung over the Fair during the 1940 season, and with the closing of the exhibits, the line returned to its usual traffic flow; the Fair sidings were ripped out in 1941-42 and routine operation marked the final seven years.

*Looking east along old Strongs Causeway towards Flushing, before it became Horace Harding Blvd. Vincent F. Seyfried collection.*

# JUNCTION AVENUE

Junction Ave. remained to the end the most picturesque Brooklyn City R.R. operation in Queens. At the turn of the century the east side of the avenue was in a stage of rapid development, the real estate operator, Jere Johnson, having opened the tract and christened it as "Louona Park" in May 1893. The west side of the street north from the L.I.R.R. tracks was a group of vast farms all of them in the hands of various members of the old and wealthy Leverich family. In 1910 Roosevelt Ave. was laid out and in 1913-14 the elevated itself was constructed eastward. Trains began running as far east as 104th St., Corona, on May 21, 1917 and thereafter home building increased rapidly through Elmhurst, East Elmhurst and Corona.

In the early 1920's the lower end of Junction Ave. from Corona Ave. to Jackson's Mill Rd. was fairly solidly lined with the two-story frame houses so typical of 1920's construction throughout Queens. The north end remained unchanged almost until the mid-30's. The trolley right-of-way itself here is an interesting story. When the line had been constructed in 1893, the only public highway in this area had been the meandering Bowery Bay Rd. Rather than purchase a long and expensive private right-of-way, the Brooklyn City used Bowery Bay Rd. all the way to North Beach. In 1915 the city adopted the "final" map of Queens, showing streets laid on the grid system. During the 1920's and 1930's the new streets were rapidly opened up on either side of the old road, which meandered back and forth

The meeting of lines. No 8433 on the Junction Ave. line and No 8345 on the Flushing-Ridgewood line, April 2, 1949. *Edward Watson collection.*

Car No 8485 on Junction Ave., April 2, 1949. *Edward Watson collection.*

B&QT sweeper No 9846 at Corona and Junction Aves., February 21, 1947. *Vincent F. Seyfried collection.*

generally between 94th St. and 97th St. The Brooklyn City, rather than negotiate a new franchise, let things stay as they were, and the local residents became accustomed to having the local trolley cut across lawns and through back yards.

By the mid-1930's all other sections of the Old Bowery Bay Rd. had disappeared; only the trolley tracks served to preserve about a mile of the old alignment. In the 1940's the city put a half-hearted top dressing along the tracks and residents used the right-of-way as a convenient street. In parts houses were built abutting the line and the road here was incorporated on the map under the new name of "Jackson's Mill Rd." To this day nearly all the right-of-way is intact and bids fair to remain. Thus quite accidentally the Junction Ave. trolley has preserved one of the original colonial highways of Queens County.

For many years "2700" series cars gave base service to North Beach; service was frequent in summer but only half-hourly in winter. In 1909 "6000" series trailers were hitched onto "4100's" of the Grand St. line and run empty to North Beach to break them in. In regular service these "6000" series cars were used only on the Flushing Ave. line west of Maspeth. In 1920 the Junction Ave. segment in winter was one of the small outlying

Car No 8312 on Junction Ave., April 2, 1949. *Edward Watson collection.*

Car No 8083 on Junction Ave., note the North Beach Airport Sign, April 2, 1949. *Edward Watson collection.*

Prohibition killed off much of the trade but a few concessions lingered on catering to a family trade. The last amusements appear to have disappeared about 1927-29 when the Grand Pier area was sold for the Glen Curtis Airport.

In 1927 a new trolley terminal was established just north of what is now the Grand Central Parkway; at the same time the

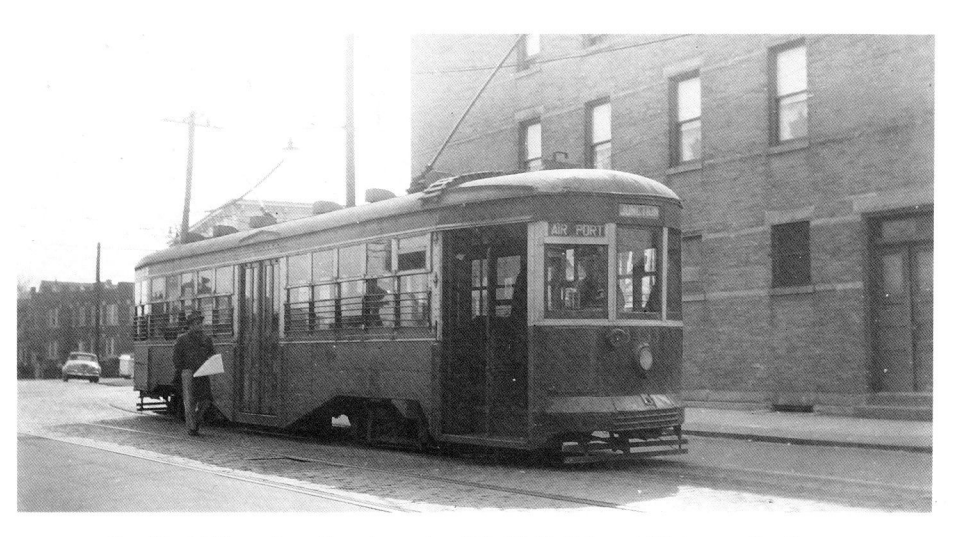

lines to be assigned Birney cars. Before these were put on, old single-truck cars were tested on the run to see whether the rails would take four-wheel cars. They did!

Although the picturesque features of private right-of-way running through the rear yards of suburban homes and down tree-arched lanes remained to the end, much of the rural appeal of the lines was lost with the disappearance of North Beach. From 1886 to the early 20's North Beach had been a miniature Coney Island, offering a 10 block stretch of Ferris wheels, shooting galleries, restaurants, beer halls, casinos, etc.

Car No 8433 on Junction Ave., April 2, 1949. *Edward Watson collection.*

tracks were relocated from the old bed of Old Bowery Bay Rd. to the center of the street at the corner of Junction Ave. and Jackson's Mill Rd. In 1929 the disused North Beach loop, consisting of 643 feet of track, was taken up altogether. In September 1937 the Federal Government authorized the Works Progress Administration to construct La Guardia Airport. Steamshovels appeared on the airport site in the fall of 1938 and began cutting down the former 53 ft. bluff to nearly sea level. In doing so, the workers approached closer and closer to the small trolley loop constructed in 1927 as the Junction Ave. terminus. The B.M.T., determined to protect its franchise, ordered one of its motormen to crash the WPA barrier erected across its own rails and ran a "2700" car right to the edge of the bluff, almost eaten away by WPA work crews. For the next three weeks relays of motormen manned the car through Christmas week of 1938 and through January 1939 until an agreement was reached with the city and Federal Governments.

*Above:* A 1923 view of the west side of 94th. St., the reverse curve is just south of Ditmars Blvd., and the private right of way along old Bowery Bay Rd. You are looking south down old Bowery Bay Rd. near Jackson's Mill Bridge. This is 23rd. Ave. today.
*Below:* Old Bowery Bay Rd. and the Abraham Rapelje farmstead, built shortly after 1724. Looking north from 23rd. Ave., just before Jackson's Mill Rd. Both photos, *Vincent F. Seyfried collection.*

**Car #2520 exiting Jackson Mill Rd. onto Astoria Blvd.** *Sidney Silleck photo.*

**Looking north up Old Bowery Bay Rd. near 24th Ave. Car No 8525, March 14, 1948.** *Sidney Silleck collection.*

**Car No 2714 on Junction Ave., looking north from Astoria Blvd. up Old Bowery Bay RD., about 1930.** *Sidney Silleck collection.*

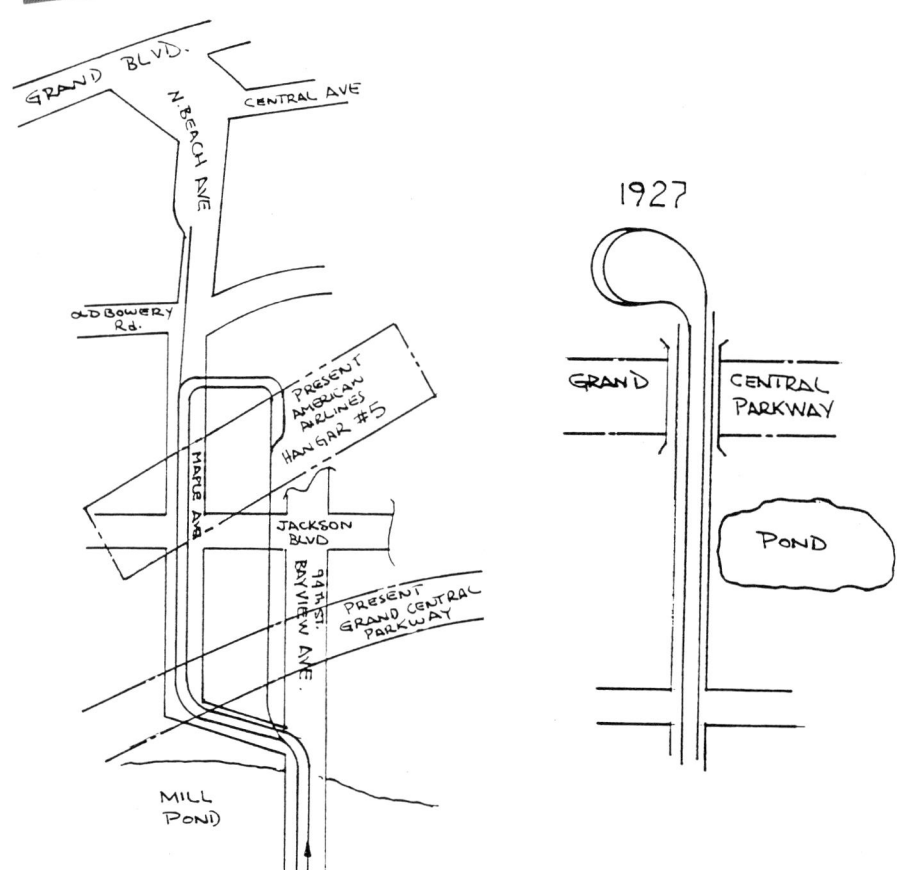

*Above Left:* Looking north up Junction Blvd. from the IRT station on Roosevelt Ave. August 1949.
*Above Right:* Looking south down Junction Blvd. from the IRT station. August 1949.
*Center:* Roosvelt Ave. IRT elevated line station at Junction Blvd, with Grand St. car No 3355 passing under. Early 1920's.
All photos, *Vincent F. Seyfried collection.*

As a result of the agreement the Junction Ave. line was cut back still further to a terminus astride the Junction Ave. bridge over Grand Central Parkway, and here it remained to the end.

For many years the line to North Beach was operated as a part of the Grand St. line, in fact, ever since the reshuffling of routes in 1899. Thirty years later, on April 7, 1929, Junction Ave. was set up as a separate line, running between North Beach and Corona Ave. This was the time the "2700's" began to be the regular cars on the route. The separate operation continued until Dec. 31, 1936 when Junction Ave. again became a part of the Grand St. route. Ten years more passed and on Feb. 6, 1946 the two lines were separated again. This time the separation remained permanent.

It is interesting to note in passing that a small part of the Junction Ave. route was shared by the New York & Queens County Ry. briefly. This was at the time that Junction Ave. was the terminus on the Corona elevated line and New York & Queens Co. cars were run in from Flushing to pick up and discharge passengers at the elevated terminus. The agreement lasted from May 15, 1923 until Oct. 29, 1925. A connecting curve was laid at Northern Blvd. and Junction Ave. and College Point and Jamaica cars came down Junction Ave. and switched back on a crossover just south of Roosevelt Ave.

## GRAND STREET

The Grand Street line within Queens County and even inside Brooklyn saw little or no changes during the last years. It will be remembered that when the Brooklyn City R.R. took over the operation of its Grand St. line in October 1919, the line was divided into two fare zones with the boundary at Newtown Creek. On Thursday, April 15, 1920, the fare zone boundary was moved eastward to 74th St., Maspeth. This change was made at the request of the Maspeth Civic Association which had filed a petition with the P.S.C. signed by over 200 residents. The Brooklyn City R.R., after long study, agreed to the change. Passengers on the Flushing Avenue line eastbound were permitted to get continuing trip tickets for rides on Grand St. or Flushing-Ridgewood cars as far east as 74th St. For passengers traveling west on Flushing or Grand St. cars, the westerly limit of the fare zones remained at Onderdonk Ave. and Newtown Creek respectively.

Car No 8477 on Metropolitan Ave. as seen looking east from the bridge overpass. *Vincent F. Seyfried collection.*

Car No 6027 at the intersection of Flushing and Metropolitan Aves., April 10, 1948. *Vincent F. Seyfried collection.*

## METROPOLITAN AVENUE

It will be recalled that the big strike of August 1920 all but killed the Metropolitan Ave. line. So poor had been the revenue from operation that the receiver had to be pressured into reopening the route. On Nov. 1, 1920 the line had been reluctantly reopened from Flushing Ave. through Middle Village to Dry Harbor Rd. and was little more than a shuttle operation serving the Myrtle Ave. elevated terminus at Lutheran Cemetery. On March 18, 1921 the line had been extended from Dry Harbor Rd. to Jamaica Ave.; finally, on April 6, 1922 the whole line was restored. When service reopened, the Myrtle Ave. el was made the zone limit; in the 1930's when home building had greatly boomed the east end of the route, the P.S.C. authorized establishment of a new zone boundary at Woodhaven Blvd. on June 25, 1934.

Up to the year 1920 most of the traffic on the Metropolitan Ave. line had been cemetery patronage; the Lutheran and St. John's cemeteries attracted heavy summer riding but the line lost money heavily throughout the other eight months of the year. The 1920's and 1930's changed all that. From Cooper Ave. eastward to Jamaica Ave. row upon row of new homes were built and many new streets opened through the section called Forest Hills and Parkville (formerly Hopedale). In Kew Gardens apartment houses sprang up, attracted by the beauties of Forest Park. The result was an enormous and welcome increase in

Car No 8458 at the Myrtle Ave. terminus at Jamaica Ave., 1949. *Vincent F. Seyfried collection.*

riding during the 1930's. Between 1922 and 1928 riding on the Metropolitan Ave. line increased at the phenomenal rate of one million each year! During 1928, 1929 and 1930 patronage remained steady at nine million per year and then very slowly declined until 1935, when another increase set in lasting through World War II.

Changes during the last 30 years in operation and trackage were small. Early in the 20's the Newtown Creek dock property was disposed of. In 1922-23 the overhead was removed and in 1925 the dock itself was sold. Dock trackage was taken out in 1926 (.325 m.) and the overhead and rails on Varick Ave. went in 1929-31. In 1925 the Juniper Ave. (69th St.) siding was taken out where cars going only as far as the el terminal had laid up, and some time during the same year the Dry Harbor Rd. spur was torn out (1,061 Ft.) at St. John's Cemetery.

The Brooklyn end of the line was curtailed at the same time. The Metropolitan shuttle, operating from Marcy Ave. to the old ferry, was discontinued on June 15, 1919, and the .6 m. of track in Metropolitan Ave. was torn out in 1929. In 1931 the whole operation along Metropolitan Ave. west of the Newtown Creek Bridge was junked, and in 1933 the rails were torn up between the bridge and Bushwick Ave. During 1933-34 a whole new bidge was built over the creek, a large concrete structure, multi-laned, and high level. All new approaches were built and all new tracks installed on both the Metropolitan Ave. and Grand St. lines for two blocks in either direction.

Metropolitan Ave. during the 20's and early 30's was frequently in the news because of the bad paving along long stretches of the road and the many floods that developed after heavy rainstorms. As late as 1930 much of the road had no blacktop pavement; the cobblestones between the rails offered the solidest roadbed, and ruts and dust holes occupied the shoulders on either side. The two worst floodbowls were at Dry Harbor Rd. and at Ascan Ave. In March 1926 the Ridgewood-Metropolitan Civic Associations complained about the poor service; the B.M.T. replied that the service would not improve until the Queens Borough President's office secured the necessary appropriation to install drains. Every time it rained, the water got so deep around Dry Harbor Rd. that the cars would not pass, and pasengers were compelled to get out and walk a quarter mile around the "pond" to board another car.

In April 1927 conditions were again bad enough to warrant a P.S.C. investigation. Residents charged that the one-man cars were the principal cause of delay because the operator had to do too many things and so kept a line of patrons waiting for admittance while he counted change, changed the pole, etc. After being haled before the commission, the B.M.T. improved the service by about 35% and an inspector was detailed to assist in maintaining the headway. More important, a crossover was

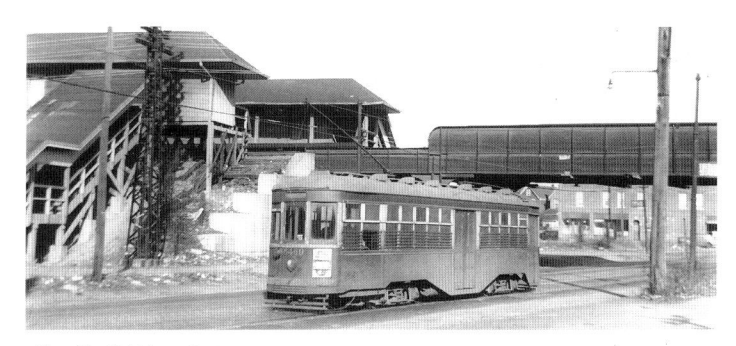

Car No 8460 at the L.I.R.R. Parkside Station, 1944. *Vincent F. Seyfried collection.*

Car No 4566 at 69th Ave. and Metropolitan Ave., just east of the L.I.R.R. Parkside Station, 1932. *Vincent F. Seyfried collection.*

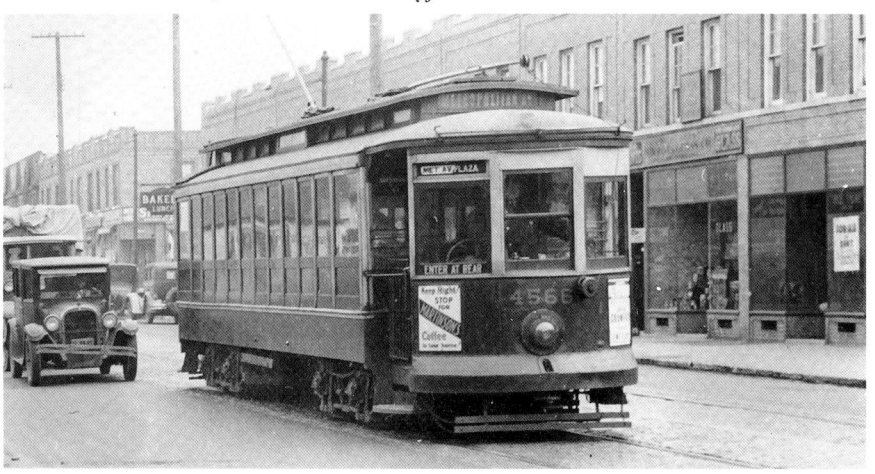

installed at 72nd Rd. to enable trolleys stalled in rainy weather by the large pool one block east of Ascan Ave. to switch back and return, maintaining two track operation on either side of the blockage.

In 1937, in answer to persistent demands of long standing, the B.M.T. extended the Metropolitan Ave. line from Jamaica Ave. out to 168th St., Jamaica. The Jamaica shopping area exercised a strong attraction for the many residents east of Cooper Ave. for whom it was the nearest big center. This made the through line from the Bridge Plaza to Jamaica one of the longest on the B.M.T. surface system - 9.21 miles. The only bad feature of the extension to Jamaica was the lack of an offstreet terminal at 169th St. Instead of one or two trolleys in the middle of the narrow street, there were now often three, an obstruction to street traffic and a source of annoyance to pedestrians and autoists. Abandonment of the Jamaica Ave. line on Nov. 30, 1947 returned the terminal to Jamaica Ave.

## RICHMOND HILL

The passing years touched Myrtle Ave. very lightly, possibly because the line traversed an older section where boom times had come decades earlier. The western end at Ridgewood attained full development before World War I and a ride from Wyckoff Ave. as far east as Fresh Pond Rd. during the early 20's would reveal the same stores and cream-brick dwellings present in 1914. Eastward through Glendale it was a different story. In and around Cooper Ave. dozens of new private homes sprang up along the north side of the street. The long stretch of Forest Park precluded much change, but at the Richmond Hill end, home construction continued the intensive start made in the middle 90's. On the whole, the Richmond Hill line traversed a very clean, prosperous area full of open park and cemetery land that redeemed the dull Ridgewood city operation with an air of lightness and suburban spaciousness.

It was just after World War I that the big car barn complex at Ridgewood began to go out of use. The first to pass was the old Bushwick R.R. barn along the north side of Myrtle Ave. used for years for storing obsolete and out-of-season cars. On Sept. 15, 1923 the building was consumed in a fire.

The old Brooklyn City car barns on Wyckoff Ave. lasted a few years longer, but these buildings were hardly more than two cars deep, lacked a second story and spread out over too much valuable city land. In 1934 the old barns were retired from active service and the buildings converted to commercial use. The barn still stands today, but shorn of all identifying architectual features.

One by one during the 1920's the various Queens lines had "gone one man", i.e., the service of a conductor had been dispensed with, and one man performed the double chore of collecting fares and running the car. Richmond Hill seems to have been the last Queens line to begin one-man operation in October 1931.

## CYPRESS HILLS

The Cypress Hills line was perhaps the quietest and most uneventful in Queens; its short length (1.17 m.) and the restricted area it served made it unlikely for anything of note to occur. It always was, and remained to the end, a cemetery shuttle giving access to the half dozen small burial grounds along the winding length of Cypress Hills Rd.

In 1919 the obsolete little single track cars that had lumbered along Cypress Ave. for years were replaced with the new Birney cars, and these continued on in service until July 31, 1935, on which date the Cypress Hills line was discontinued as a separate route. By this date the Cypress Hills Birneys were the last B.M.T. cars of their kind to operate in Queens County. On Aug. 1, 1935 operation of the route was taken over by cars of the Bushwick Ave. line, which was extended from the Wyckoff Ave. terminus, an arrangement that continued to the end.

Of all B.M.T. trolley routes in Queens, Cypress Hills was never rerailed! The short segment from Myrtle Ave. to Weirfield St., used by the Putnam Ave. line, had to be rebuilt in 1938, but along the remainder of the line the old tracks, ancient nine-inch, 94lb. tram rail laid in 1899, remained in use, and so far as is known, were never renewed. Curiously, no one seemed to care; no complaints about rough roadbed appeared in the newspapers, and year by year the traffic fell off. From 1909 to 1919 the little line carried just over a million passengers a year; roughly 700,000 from 1920 to 1928, and barely 300,000 by 1935. By the 1940's the Cypress Hills line had shrunk into relative insignificance, as had the Bushwick Ave. route operating over it.

B&QT No 8270 at Park Lane South, Forest Park. *William Meyers photo.*

82

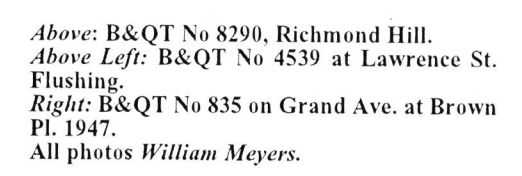

*Above*: B&QT No 8290, Richmond Hill.
*Above Left:* B&QT No 4539 at Lawrence St. Flushing.
*Right:* B&QT No 835 on Grand Ave. at Brown Pl. 1947.
All photos *William Meyers*.

*Right:* **Terminus of the Richmond Hill line at Jamaica and Myrtle Ave.**
*Below Left:* **Car #8431 at the terminus of the Metropolitan Ave. line at Jamaica Ave., 1948.**
*Below Right:* **Looking west along Metropolitan Ave. from the former Parkside station on the LIRR Rockaway line, June 10, 1949.**
All photos *Vincent Seyfried.*

# THE END

One might say that the trolley era came to an end in June 1940. For decades previously the city and the B.M.T. had been associated in the construction of many rapid transit projects and extensions, and it had always been a cardinal point of city policy that ownership of these routes should be vested in the city, though operation was leased to the B.M.T. After years of study and negotiations the three great city transit systems, namely, the Brooklyn-Manhattan Co., the Interborough Rapid Transit Co., and the city owned Independent system were all purchased and unified into one vast, complex system, the operation and management of which was entrusted to the Board of Transportation. Since the Brooklyn surface routes were all subsidiaries of the B.M.T., the vast Brooklyn trolley system was transferred to municipal ownership and management as part of the deal.

The old B.M.T. management had always been strongly trolley-minded; indeed, the B.M.T. had pioneered in the development of the modern P.C.C. car, and many of the experiments were conducted in Brooklyn. Several studies made by the B.M.T. engineers pointed to the desirability of retaining the heavy lines as trolley routes, and eliminating the weaker feeder lines. The B.M.T.'s plans to convert the whole system gradually to P.C.C. operation were brought to an untimely end by the unification of 1940.

B&QT cars 8445 and 4539 at the World Fair loop at Lawrence St., December 28, 1947. *Vincent F. Seyfried collection.*

Looking west along Metropolitan Ave. towards the Interboro Parkway, 1949. *Vincent F. Seyfried collection.*

Junction Ave. line car No 8499 sits on the overpass atop Grand Central Parkway, at the La Guardia Airport end of the line. The American Airline hangars are in the backround. *Vincent F. Seyfried collection.*

*B&QT car No 8439 in Flushing, 1958. William Meyers photo.*

It was not long before trolley abandonment became the order of the day. For a year or more the Board of Transportation took no firm policy stand; then in 1941 the decision was taken for gradual motorization. Five lines were motorized in 1941 and three in 1942. The outbreak of war in December 1941 destroyed plans for further substitution and trolleys continued to operate on the remaining lines.

The war years were hard on the surface lines. Repair parts were hard to get, labor turnover was high, and near-suppression of private auto driving threw thousands more riders onto the overcrowded cars. Many trolleys unused for a decade and ready for the scrap heap were pressed back into service. The tracks and overhead received almost no regular maintenance. At the end of the war the trolley fleet itself was largely obsolete; only 100 P.C.C. cars were in service and the base service "8000" series was 20 to 25 years old; the "6000's", 15 years old. Tradition was all against street car replacement. The administration of Hylan and La Guardia had been vehemently anti-trolley; there were also arguments about traffic obstruction, slow acceleration, noise, etc. The most potent reason was certainly economic,

soaring cost of labor making track replacement prohibitive. The new P.C.C. trolleys themselves with electronic refinements tended to price themselves out of the market. With the appointment of Sidney H. Bingham as Chairman of the Board of Transportation in May 1947, the motorization program picked up speed. Mr. Bingham was a designer of buses and had many ties with the manufacturers. Nine abandonments took place in 1947, the largest number to date; among these were the Cypress Hills line on Sept. 1, 1947 and the Jamaica Ave. line on Nov. 30, 1947.

The year 1948 saw only five abandonments because of delays in delivery of new buses and difficulties in the financing of such large scale capital replacements. One of these was Flushing Ave., replaced by trolley buses on Nov. 21, 1948. The year 1949 saw the end of all remaining trolley operations in Queens County. First to be replaced was the Metropolitan Ave. line. On midnight June 12th, 37 buses replaced 24 trolleys along the route, which received the designation B-53. There was no special ceremony, but members of the Middle Village Property Owner's Association were invited to ride the first bus. Next to go was the Flushing-Ridgewood line the last car #8435 left Ridgewood on Sunday, July 17th, at 4:02 a.m. for Flushing; it departed from Main St., Flushing, at 4:48 a.m. and returned to its barn in Ridgewood at 5:35 a.m. The first bus started for Ridgewood from the Maspeth depot at 4:10 a.m. Slightly more publicity was given to this occasion. The "Long Island Star Journal" sent a reporter to snap the last car, but because of the lateness of the hour, the reporter casually snapped the first passing car and the bus he saw, and the falsified photo duly appeared the following day on the front page as the "last" car and "first" bus.

For a month the abandonment of the Flushing-Ridgewood operation left Junction Ave. isolated, but not for long. On Aug. 25, 1949 buses displaced the trolleys along Junction Ave. Since portions of the Old Bowery Bay Rd. north of Astoria Blvd. were impassable for the new buses, 94th St. was substituted instead.

On Dec. 11, 1949 the Grand St. line, the oldest of the B.R.T. lines on the north side of the county, succumbed to the new order. Thirteen new buses replaced the 12 trolley cars on the route. As usual, the substitution was quiet and uneventful. Richmond Hill was the last of the Queens lines to go on April 26, 1950.

Although the familiar red cars that had operated along Queens streets for so many years were a thing of the past by 1950, the rails remained for some years longer as a reminder of the old order of things. In the first week of June 1951 removal of the car tracks was begun along Metropolitan Ave. from Jamaica Ave. to Union Tpk. at a cost of $151,275. On June 15, 1951 track removal was begun on Myrtle Ave. from Cypress St. to the Brooklyn line

86

at a cost to the city of $120,413. In March 1952 approximately 10,000 steel trolley poles along Metropolitan Ave. were removed; this time the contractor paid the city $80,591 for the scrap metal.

After a three-year lapse the city awarded another $63,774 contract to remove 3,000 ft. of rail along Myrtle Ave. from Cypress Hills St. to 71st St. Thereafter the policy of actual physical removal of the rails was changed to the cheaper method of paving directly over the rails. The whole Cypress Hills line, most of Junction Ave., all Grand St., all Fresh Pond Rd. and 61st St., and three miles of Myrtle Ave. from 80th St. to Jamaica Ave. were simply covered over with fresh blacktop to hide the trolley rails; most of this work was done from August to November 1956. At the present the sole surviving trolley rails of the old B.M.T. system in Queens that can still be seen thru sections of pavement are along the former private right-of-way on the Old Bowery Bay Rd. where they bother no one.

Thus has the hand of time effectively obliterated the reminders of a proud past. Today the city's green and silver buses operate all the former trolley routes, and only the older generation preserves the memory of a more leisurely day when houses in Queens were few, and the trolley the sole thread that linked communities whose individuality had been completely effaced by the sea of houses covering every part of Queens borough.

The private right of way, Old Bowery Bay Rd., as it is today. *William Meyers photo.*

Under the Myrtle Ave. Elevated today. *William Meyers photo.*

87

# BROOKLYN RAPID TRANSIT ROSTER-1920
## Compiled by Edward B. Watson June 1952

| Car No. | Builder | Year | Owner | Car Type |
|---|---|---|---|---|
| 1-8 | L&F | 1890 | BHRR | Semi-Conv |
| 14-16 | L&F | 1890 | BHRR | Open-8 Bnch |
| 17-19 | JCC | 1890 | BCRR | Open-8 Bnch |
| 100-103 | PCC | 1893 | BCRR | Closed |
| 104-117 | SLC | 1893 | BCRR | Closed |
| 118-138 | L&F | 1894 | BCRR | Closed |
| 139-151 | JGB | 1894 | BCRR | Closed |
| 152-160 | SLC | 1894 | BCRR | Closed |
| 161-162 | L&F | 1894 | BQCS | Closed |
| 163-168 | STP | 1895 | NERR | Closed |
| 169-176 | SLC | 1895 | NERR | Closed |
| 177, 179 | L&F | 1894 | BCRR | Closed |
| 178, 187 | JGB | 1894 | BCRR | Closed |
| 180-182 | L&F | 1894 | BCRR | Closed |
| 183 | SLC | 1895 | BCRR | Closed |
| 184-186 | L&F | 1894 | BCRR | Closed |
| 188-189 | SLC | 1894 | BCRR | Closed |
| 190 | L&F | 1894 | NERR | Closed |
| 192-194 | BRN | 1895 | NERR | Closed |
| 200-299 | STP | 1898 | BCRR | Open-12 Bnch |
| 300-369 | STP | 1898 | BCRR | Closed |
| 370-399 | SLC | 1898 | BCRR | Closed |
| 400-419 | BHR | 1898 | BCRR | Open-12 Bnch |
| 420-454 | JGB | 1899 | BCRR | Open-13 Bnch |
| 455-499 | JGB | 1899 | NERR | Open-13 Bnch |
| 500-509 | LAC | 1897 | BCRR | Closed |
| 510-529 | SLC | 1897 | BCRR | Closed |
| 530-549 | JGB | 1897 | BCRR | Closed |
| 550-554 | LAC | 1897 | BCRR | Closed |
| 555-579 | AMC | 1898 | BCRR | Closed |
| 600-674 | SLC | 1899 | BCRR | Open-13 Bnch |
| 675-699 | BRG | 1899 | BCRR | Open-13 Bnch |
| 700-714 | BNY | 1896 | BCRR | Closed |
| 715-749 | B&S | 1896 | BCRR | Closed |
| 750 | BHR | 1896 | BCRR | Closed |
| 751-755 | LAC | 1897 | BCRR | Closed |
| 756-760 | SLC | 1898 | BCRR | Closed |
| 761-770 | AMC | 1898 | BCRR | Closed |
| 771-785 | SLC | 1898 | BCRR | Closed |
| 786 | STP | 1898 | BCRR | Closed |
| 787-795 | JGB | 1898 | BCRR | Conv. |
| 796-797 | B&S | 1894 | BCRR | Conv. |
| 798 | JGB | 1895 | BCRR | Conv. |
| 799 | JGB | 1897 | CIBR | Closed |

| Car No | Builder | Year | Owner | Car Type |
|---|---|---|---|---|
| 800-849 | AMC | 1900 | NERR | Open-13 Bnch |
| 850-899 | B&S | 1900 | NERR | Open-13 Bnch |
| 900-909 | JGB | 1896 | CIBR | Closed |
| 910-919 | JGB | 1897 | CIBR | Closed |
| 920-999 | JGB | 1898 | CIBR | Closed |
| 1000-1099 | AMC | 1900 | NERR | Open-13 Bnch |
| 1100-1128* | JGB | 1899 | CIBR | Closed |
| 1129-1178* | JGB | 1903 | CIBR | Closed |
| 1200-1299* | LAC | 1900 | NERR | Open-13 Bnch |
| 1400-1449 | STP | 1901 | NERR | Open-13 Bnch |
| 1450-1499 | STP | 1902 | BOCS | Open-13 Bnch |
| 1600-1649 | STP | 1902 | BOCS | Open-13 Bnch |
| 1650-1659 | JGB | 1897 | CIBR | Open-12 Bnch |
| 1660-1699 | JGB | 1898 | CIBR | Open-12 Bnch |
| 1700-1739 | SLC | 1899 | BCRR | Closed |
| 1740-1749 | SLC | 1899 | NERR | Closed |
| 1750-1799 | LAC | 1899 | NERR | Closed |
| 1800-1899 | JGB | 1898 | CIBR | Open-12 Bnch |
| 1900-1949 | AMC | 1899 | NERR | Closed |
| 2000-2009 | JGB | 1898 | CIBR | Open-12 Bnch |
| 2010-2058 | JGB | 1899 | CIBR | Open-12 Bnch |
| 2059-2099 | JGB | 1904 | CIBR | Open-13 Bnch |
| 2100-2174* | LAC | 1899 | NERR | Closed |
| 2175-2199 | BRG | 1899 | NERR | Closed |
| 2200-2208 | JGB | 1904 | CIBR | Open-13 Bnch |
| 2380-2389* | JGB | 1905 | CIBR | Semi-Conv. |
| 2390-2399 | JGB | 1907 | CIBR | Semi-Conv. |
| 2400-2449 | SLC | 1898 | NERR | Open-10 Bnch |
| 2450-2499 | JGB | 1896 | NERR | Open-10 Bnch |
| 2500-2599* | STP | 1907 | TDC | Semi-Conv. |
| 2600-2604* | JGB | 1896 | NERR | Open-10 Bnch |
| 2605-2620* | SLC | 1897 | NERR | Open-10 Bnch |
| 2621-2641 | JGB | 1896 | NERR | Open-10 Bnch |
| 2642-2661 | NER | 1898 | NERR | Open-10 Bnch |
| 2662 | JGB | 1896 | NERR | Open-9 Bnch |
| 2700-2704 | BHR | 1901 | NERR | Semi-Conv. |
| 2705-2754* | LAC | 1901 | BCRR | Semi-Conv. |
| 2755-2799 | LAC | 1902 | NERR | Semi-Conv. |
| 2900-2904 | LAC | 1902 | NERR | Semi-Conv. |
| 2905-2954* | STP | 1902 | NERR | Semi-Conv. |
| 2955-2999* | LAC | 1902 | BQCS | Semi-Conv. |
| 3100-3154* | LAC | 1902 | BQCS | Semi-Conv. |
| 3155-3199 | STP | 1903 | TDC | Semi-Conv. |
| 3300-3304* | STP | 1903 | TDC | Semi-Conv. |
| 3305-3354* | KUL | 1904 | TDC | Semi-Conv. |

| Car No. | Builder | Year | Owner | Car Type |
|---|---|---|---|---|
| 3355-3399 | STP | 1904 | TDC | Semi-Conv. |
| 3500-3554 | STP | 1904 | TDC | Semi-Conv. |
| 3555 | STP | 1905 | NERR | Conv. |
| 3556 | PSC | 1906 | NERR | Conv. |
| 3557 | SSC | 1912 | NERR | Cent.Ent. |
| 3700-3736* | JGB | 1905 | BQCS | Conv. |
| 3737-3753* | JGB | 1905 | NERR | Conv. |
| 3754-3758 | JGB | 1905 | BQCS | Conv. |
| 3759-3768 | JGB | 1905 | NERR | Conv. |
| 3769-3799 | JGB | 1905 | BCRR | Conv. |
| 3900-3924 | JGB | 1905 | NERR | Conv. |
| 3925-3974 | STP | 1905 | NERR | Conv. |
| 3975-3999 | JWT | 1905 | NERR | Conv. |
| 4100 | STP | 1906 | NERR | Conv. |
| 4101-4199 | STP | 1906 | NERR | Conv. |
| 4300-4349 | LAC | 1906 | TDC | Conv. |
| 4500-4549 | JWT | 1906 | TDC | Conv. |
| 4550-4574 | LAC | 1906 | TDC | Conv. |
| 4575-4599 | LAC | 1906 | CIGR | Conv. |
| 4900 | STL | 1915 | Cnv to Articulated Car Ex. 167-168 | |
| 5000-5099 | JGB | 1913 | TDC | Cent.Ent. |
| 6000-6053 | JGB | 1919 | BHRR | Tra/Er |
| 6054-6090 | JGB | 1919 | NERR | Tra/Er |
| 6091-6095 | JGB | 1919 | CIBR | Tra/Er |
| 6096-6099 | JGB | 1919 | BOCS | Tra/Er |
| 7000-7107 | JGB | 1919 | BCRR | Birney |
| 7108-7180 | JGB | 1919 | NERR | Birney |
| 7181-7191 | JGB | 1919 | CIBR | Birney |
| 7192-7199 | JGB | 1919 | BQCS | Birney |
| 7200-7205 | CINI | 1919 | SBRR | Birney |
| 8000-8099* | JGB | 1923 | BCRR | Peter Witt |
| 8100-8199* | SLC | 1923 | BCRR | Peter Witt |
| 8200-8299 | SLC | 1925 | BCRR | Peter Witt |
| 8300-8399* | JGB | 1925 | BCRR | Peter Witt |
| 8400-8449 | JGB | 1925 | BCRR | Peter Witt |
| 8450-8499 | OGB | 1925 | BCRR | Peter Witt |
| 8500-8534 | OGB | 1925 | BCRR | Peter Witt |
| 1001-1099 | SLC | 1936 | | PCC |

**Bridge Operating Company Cars**
(Built for Operation on Williamsburg Bridge)

| | | | | |
|---|---|---|---|---|
| 1-20 | JWT | 1905 | BO Co. | Closed |

*Series Used Generally on Jamaica Avenue Line after 1905.

**Builders**

| | |
|---|---|
| AMC | American Car Co. |
| BHR | Brooklyn Hgts RR |
| BNY | Brooklyn & NYRR Supply Co. |
| BRG | Briggs Car Co. |
| BRN | Brownell |
| B&S | Barney & Smith |
| CIN | Cinncinatti Car Co. |
| JCC | Jones Car Co. |
| JWT | Jewett Car Co. |
| KUL | Kuhlman Car Co. |
| LAC | Laclede Car Co. |
| L&F | Lewis & Fowler |
| NER | Nassau Elec R. R. |
| OGB | Osgood Bradley |
| PCC | Pullman Car Co. |
| PSC | Pressed Steel Car Co. |
| SLC | St.Louis Car Co. |
| SSC | Standard Steel Car Co |
| STP | John Stephenson Co. |

**Owning Companies**

| | |
|---|---|
| BCRR | Brooklyn City RR |
| BHRR | Brooklyn Heights RR |
| BQCS | Brooklyn Queens Co. & Suburban RR |
| CIBR | Coney Isl & Bklyn RR |
| CIGR | Coney Island & Gravesend RR |
| NERR | Nassau Electric RR |
| SBRR | South Brooklyn Ry Co. |
| TDC | Transit Development Co. |